DANIEL

Martin Buber

DANIEL

DIALOGUES ON REALIZATION

Translated
with an
Introductory Essay
by
MAURICE
FRIEDMAN

HOLT,
RINEHART
AND
WINSTON
New York
Chicago
San Francisco

Published in German under the title *Daniel, Die Gespräche von der
Verwirklichung,* by Insel-Verlag, Leipzig.

Author's Preface from Martin Buber, *Werke,* Vol. I, *Schriften zur
Philosophie.* Kösel-Verlag, Munich; Verlag Lambert Schneider,
Heidelberg, 1962, page 11.

Published simultaneously in Canada by Holt, Rinehart
and Winston of Canada, Limited.

First Edition

Library of Congress Catalog Card Number: 64–14363

81119-0114

Printed in the United States of America

Acknowledgments

I am grateful to Professor Buber for his suggestions concerning my Introduction and translation.

I also wish to acknowledge my gratitude to the following publishers who have so generously granted permission to reprint from their publications:

New Directions, for excerpts from "Fern Hill," from *The Collected Poems of Dylan Thomas*. Copyright 1953 by Dylan Thomas, © 1957 by New Directions.

W. W. Norton & Company, Inc., for excerpts from *Duino Elegies* by Rainer Maria Rilke. English translation by J. B. Leishman and Stephen Spender. Copyright, 1939, by W. W. Norton & Co., Inc., New York, N. Y.

CONTENTS

Translator's Preface

For many years Martin Buber refused to permit the publication of an English translation of his early poetical-philosophical work Daniel *on the grounds that it did not represent his mature thought as that has developed from* I and Thou *onward. Finally, under the urging of Arthur A. Cohen and myself, he consented, provided, he stipulated, that I "write an introduction explaining, even at some length, that this is an early book in which there is already expressed the great duality of human life, but only in its cognitive and not yet in its communicative and existential character. This book is obviously a book of transition to a new kind of thinking and must be characterized as such."*

Since this is so, the question arises, Why is it desirable to publish this early work? The answer is fivefold. First, Martin Buber's stature in the world of letters today is so great that it is of real value that readers should be in a position to glean the added understanding that inevitably comes from reading a transitional work which shows how he moved to his philosophy of dialogue. Second, there are many elements in Daniel *that have remained, albeit in more sober form, in Buber's later thought. Third,* Daniel, *better*

ix

than any other single work, enables us to understand the significance of the transition Buber made from his early mysticism to his later philosophy of dialogue and the sense in which he did and did not retain elements of mystic immediacy and presentness even when he decisively discarded his philosophy of unity through realization for his philosophy of meeting what is over against us. Fourth, Daniel *adds to an understanding of an atmosphere of style and spirit that Buber shared with Rainer Maria Rilke and Hugo von Hofmannsthal, and it had, as we shall see, a direct influence on one of Rilke's* Duino Elegies. *Fifth, and most important of all, while some of* Daniel *seems definitely dated, not only in thought but in spirit and style, much of it is still of genuine value both as literature and philosophy. Now that Martin Buber's I-Thou philosophy is too well known for anyone to confuse Buber's life of dialogue with mystical union, we can safely appreciate what in* Daniel *may speak to our condition and even use it as a stepping-stone to the more mature but, by the same token, more condensed poetical-philosophical classic* I and Thou.

Maurice Friedman
Professor of Philosophy
Sarah Lawrence College

Bronxville, New York
October, 1963

DANIEL

Translator's Introduction

Martin Buber's *Daniel* was first published in 1913 by Insel Verlag, Leipzig, Germany. Although it is an early work, it is also the culmination of an important sequence in Buber's thought from his earliest essays in 1900 and 1901 up to the time of its publication.

The Cultural Background of Daniel

Although Buber goes far beyond transcendental idealism, he still starts with Kant's teaching that we ourselves impose the order of space and time upon experience to enable us to orient ourselves in it. From Kant, Buber says, he gained an inkling "that being itself was beyond the reach alike of the finitude and the infinity of space and time, since it only appeared in space and time but did not itself enter into this appearance." But the problem that Buber faced and that he inherited from the age when idealism had begun to break up was that of how man can reach "reality" without returning to the naïve, pre-Kantian "objective" view of the universe.

Buber found this reality through perceiving that in addition to man's orienting function he also possesses a "realizing" function which brings him into real contact with God, with other men, and with nature. The thought of his teacher, Wilhelm Dilthey, provided an important bridge to this philosophy of "realization," for Dilthey based his thought on the radical difference between the way of knowing proper to the *Geisteswissenschaften*—the humane studies such as philosophy, the social sciences, and psychology—and that proper to the *Naturwissenschaften*—the natural sciences. In the former, the knower cannot be merely a detached scientific observer but must himself participate, for it is through his participation that he discovers both the typical and the unique in the aspects of human life that he is studying.

Another important influence on Buber's philosophy of realization was the thought of Friedrich Nietzsche. In one of his earliest articles (1901), Buber spoke of Nietzsche as "the first pathfinder of the new culture," "the awakener and creator of new life-values and a new world-feeling." Nietzsche's influence may account in part for the dynamism of Buber's early philosophy, for its concern with creativity and greatness, for its emphasis on the concrete and actual as opposed to the ideal and abstract, for its idea of the fruitfulness of conflict, and for its emphasis on the value of life impulses and wholeness of being as opposed to detached intellectuality.

Probably the strongest influence on Buber's concept of realization, however, was the existentialist philosophy of Søren Kierkegaard. In Kierkegaard's earlier works is found the germ of some of Buber's most important early and later ideas: the direct relation between the

4

individual and God, the insecure and exposed state of every individual as an individual, the "knight of faith" who cannot take shelter in the universal but must constantly risk all in the concrete uniqueness of each new situation, and the importance of realizing one's belief in one's life.

Buber has spoken of Kierkegaard and Dostoevski together as the two men of the nineteenth century who will, in his opinion, "remain" in the centuries to come. In Dostoevski, Buber found spiritual intensity, fervor, depth of insight, and an understanding of man's inner cleavage. He also found in him something of that dynamism and concern for realization in life that mark both Nietzsche and Kierkegaard. Finally, he found in him a dialectic very similar to his own intellectual processes and a world-affirming mystic religion of ecstasy, love, and brotherhood which bears a remarkable resemblance to his own thought.[1]

Daniel shows the influence of the religions of the Orient—in particular, Taoism, Buddhism, and the Hindu Vedanta. The influence of the more monistic religions was most important at an earlier period in the development of Buber's thought (1900–1910), but that of Taoism came slightly later and has persisted into Buber's mature philosophy. At least as important in this early period as the influence of Taoism was that of German mysticism from Meister Eckhart to Angelus Silesius. Of these mystics the two most important for Buber were Meister Eckhart, whom Buber has called "the greatest thinker of Western mysticism," and Jakob Boehme, with whose philosophy

[1] The foregoing passages are taken, with slight modification, from Maurice Friedman, Martin Buber: The Life of Dialogue (New York: Harper Torchbooks, 1960), pp. 34 ff., to which I refer the scholar for footnotes.

5

Buber found himself in close accord in the early years of this century. The dialectical attitude toward evil which informs not only Buber's early but his mature philosophy is very similar to the attitude of both Eckhart and Boehme. Moreover, these mystics provided a bridge for Buber to Jewish mysticism. The German mystical idea of the birth of the *Ungrund,* or godhead, in the soul, and the Kabbalistic and Hasidic idea of the unification of God and his exiled immanence (the Shekinah) led Buber, he says, "to the thought of the realization of God through man" which he later abandoned for the meeting of God and man.[2]

It is not Jewish mysticism in general, however, but Hasidism, the popular communal Jewish mysticism of eighteenth- and nineteenth-century East European Jewry, which had the greatest influence on the development of Buber's philosophy, and this is also evident in *Daniel.* Hasidism placed a strong emphasis on the immanence of God—not as an accomplished fact, as with pantheism, but as a task, as in panentheism. The divine in the world must be brought, through our action, to ever greater and purer might. Man has a part in the Shekinah, the exiled Glory of God, which enables him to be a co-worker with God in the perfection of the world toward redemption. Thus the stress of Hasidism is on the actual consummation of religious life—the inward experience of the presence of God and the actualization of that presence in all one's actions.

One might be tempted to think that Bergson had exercised a direct and important influence on Buber when one considers the similarity

[2] **Martin Buber,** Between Man and Man, **trans. by Ronald Gregor Smith** (Boston: Beacon Paperbacks, 1955), **"What Is Man?"** pp. 184 ff.

between Buber's early philosophy of "realization" as expressed in *Daniel* and some of Bergson's central concepts, such as "intuition," *élan vital*, and *durée*. Hans Kohn has twice stated, however, that Buber did not become acquainted with Bergson's philosophy until after he had written *Daniel*, and Professor Buber has confirmed to me directly that Bergson had no important influence on his thought. It is rather, Kohn suggests, Nietzsche's influence on both Bergson and Buber that accounts for the similarity between these two thinkers.[3] The development of Buber's thought since *Daniel* follows squarely on the basis laid in that book, with important changes only in the direction of Buber's philosophy of dialogue and, by the same token, away from some of the elements in Buber's earlier thought which had made it similar to Bergson. Bergson's intuition is a sympathy of the individual with the whole movement of life, while Buber's I-Thou relation, and even his philosophy of realization in *Daniel*, are characterized by the polar tension between two separate beings in direct relation with each other.[4]

Buber's Early Thought

Buber's early essays are a rich source for the discovery and articulation of those attitudes which have been brought to unity and relative maturity in *Daniel*. We find in them in a markedly clear fashion the concern for personal wholeness, for the realization of truth in life, and for the joining of spirit and of basic life energies which appear in

[3] **Hans Kohn,** Martin Buber, Sein Werk und seine Zeit. Ein Beitrag zur Geistesgeschichte Mitteleuropas 1880–1930. **Nachwort: 1930–1960 by Robert Weltsch. (Cologne: Joseph Melzer Verlag, 1961), pp. 21, 116.**
[4] **Cf. Buber's essay on "Bergson's Intuition" in Martin Buber,** Pointing the Way, **ed. & trans. with an Editor's Introduction by Maurice Friedman (New York: Harper Torchbooks, 1963).**

7

all Buber's later writings and which justify us in including Buber among the important religious existentialists of our age.

"Where the right dedication is, there also is the power," writes Buber in 1901. The most important manifestation of this wholeness and inwardness is found in creativity. But the truly creative person is not the intellectual, nor is he simply the artist. He is the strong and many-sided man in whom human happenings stream together in order to attain new developments in spirit and deed. The redeeming affirmation of a conflict is the essence of all creativity; in the creative person a deep inner division is brought to harmony. He is not one who passes over the abysses; rather he has seen all and received all and dares to will this foul world. Today faith has lost its power to take souls in its arms and lay them on the heart of the world, for faith lies to life and does violence to its surging meanings. Today Satan does not lead the creative man to a high mountain to show him all the kingdoms and splendor of the world. Instead he tempts him through infinity to lose himself in the inessential, to roam about in the great confusion in which all human clarity and definiteness have ceased. The creative kingdom, however, is there where form and formation thrive.[5]

The world is no being over against one, says Buber, in his 1901 essay on Jakob Boehme. It is a becoming. We do not have to accept the world as it is; we continually create it. Reality itself is new every day, and every morning it asks anew to be shaped by our hands. We create

[5] **Martin Buber,** Die jüdische Bewegung. Gesammelte Aufsätze und Ansprachen. **Vol. I, 1900-1914 (Berlin: Judischer Verlag, 1916), pp. 29, 66-73.**

the world when we unknowingly lend our perceptions the concentration and firmness that make them into a reality, when at every moment an unconscious existential judgment about things, that is, about sense impressions, speaks in us: *this is*. But deeper and more inwardly we consciously create the world by letting our strength flow into the becoming, by entering ourselves into world destiny and becoming an element in the great event, until the changes that our creation awakes have become themselves a source of numberless new and liberating sense impressions of many kinds. Thus we are not the slaves but the lovers of our world.

There are two basic forces through which all things are moved: the longing for conflict and the longing for love. The movement of conflict leads to individuation, that of love to God. Conflict develops individuality into personality; love leads the individual to reborn unity of power. This concept finds its confirmation and completion, writes Buber, in a sentence of Ludwig Feuerbach's: "Man by himself is man in the ordinary sense of the term; man with man—the unity of I and Thou—is God." Feuerbach's unity is founded on the reality of the difference between "I" and "Thou," but we stand nearer to the teaching of Boehme than to that of Feuerbach, writes Buber, to the feeling of Saint Francis of Assisi who called the trees, the birds, and the stars his brothers and sisters, and still nearer to the Vedanta. Yet the division between the "I" and the world is even at this stage a prime fact of Buber's experience. Conflict is a bridge because in it and through it one "I" reveals itself in its beauty to another "I," and love is a bridge because in it being unites itself with God. Out of the intermixture of the two comes life, in which things neither exist in rigid separation nor melt into one another, but reciprocally condition themselves. This reciprocal conditioning is bound up with the existence of all individuals.

It is not enough that the "I" unite itself with the world. The "I" is the world. This is not in the sense of Berkeley for whom the world is a succession of perceptions of an "I," nor is it in the sense of Fichte who posits the identity of the knower and the known and comprehends the world in the "I." It is rather in the sense of that great Renaissance teaching of the microcosm which has been transmitted to us through Leibniz and Goethe. "God is not divided but everywhere whole, and where he reveals himself, there is he wholly present." Heaven and earth and all creatures and even God himself lie in man.

This wonderful world-feeling, says Buber, has become wholly our own. We have woven it in our innermost experience. When I bring a piece of fruit to my mouth, I feel: this is my body; and when I set wine to my lips, I feel: this is my blood. And there often comes to us the desire to put our arms around a young tree and feel the same surge of life as in ourselves or to read our own most special mystery in the eyes of a dumb animal. We experience the ripening and fading of far-distant stars as something which happens to us, and there are moments in which our organism is wholly another piece of nature.[6]

If in this 1901 essay, the feeling of unity illustrates the idea of the microcosm, in the introduction to *Ecstatic Confessions* (1909) it illus-

[6] **Martin Buber, "Über Jakob Böhme,"** Wiener Rundschau, **Vol. V, No. 1 (June 15, 1901), pp. 251-253.**

trates the oneness in ecstasy of the "I" and the world; in *Daniel* (1913) it illustrates the unity of the world and the soul which is not found, as in ecstasy, but is created and realized in the world; while in *I and Thou* (1923) it illustrates meeting—an event which takes place between two beings who nonetheless remain separate and other.

In Hasidism, Buber claims in 1906, ecstasy is not, as in German mysticism, an "un-becoming" (*Entwerden*) of the soul but rather its unfolding; it is not the self-limiting but the self-fulfilling soul which flows into the Absolute. In asceticism the spiritual being shrinks, sleeps, becomes empty and confused; only in joy can it awaken and fulfill itself, until, free from all deficiency, it attains unto the divine.[7] In "Ecstasy and Confession," however, the introductory essay to *Ecstatic Confessions* (1909), Buber states that the ecstatic at the time of ecstasy achieves true and perfect unity in which the world and the "I" are one and all multiplicity has disappeared. Most mystics, not suspecting that their individual "I" contains the world "I," have connected their experience with God and have made of it a multiform mystery. Only in the primitive word of India is the "I" proclaimed one with the All and with the One. The unity which the ecstatic experiences when he has brought all his former multiplicity into oneness is not a relative unity, bounded by the existence of other individuals, but is without limits, for it is the absolute, unlimited oneness which includes all others. The ecstatic man no longer has others outside of himself with whom he has community. Here once again Buber speaks as a Vedantist, as an unqualified nondualist who asserts that "thou art that."

[7] **Martin Buber,** Die Geschichten des Rabbi Nachman **(Frankfurt am Main: Rutten & Loening, 1906), pp. 13 ff.**

Even though the world and "I" are one in ecstasy, the mystic must return to the world of multiplicity and attempt, however futilely, to take up his communion with those others who were at once completely united with him and completely cut off from him during his experience of ecstasy. The need of the mystic to communicate is not only weakness and stammering, says Buber, it is also power and melody. The mystic desires to create a lasting memorial of his ineffable experience of ecstasy, to bring the timeless over into time—he desires to make the unity without multiplicity into the unity of all multiplicity. This desire brings to mind the great myths of the One which becomes the many because it wishes to see and be seen, to know and be known, to love and be loved, to comprehend itself as many while remaining One—the myth of the "I" that creates a "Thou," of the primeval Self that turns itself into world, of the godhead that becomes God. Is not the experience of the ecstatic a symbol of the primeval experience of the world spirit? Are not both one experience? We turn inward and listen, and we do not know which sea's roar it is that we hear.[8]

This is a position which the Hindu Vedanta characterizes as *vishista-dvaita*, or qualified nondualism: it preserves the essential oneness of all things, yet unlike absolute nondualism it recognizes the reality of creation and of the movement of the many back to the One, of man back to God. It has much in common with Meister Eckhart and is especially close to the dialectic of Jakob Boehme, yet it is still a long way from Buber's I-Thou philosophy and is later repudiated by Buber in favor of the treatment of unity in the fifth dialogue of

[8] **Martin Buber,** Ekstatische Konfessionen **(Jena: Eugen Diedrichs Verlag, 1909),** "Ekstase und Bekenntnis," **pp. xi f., xv f., xviii, xxii-xxvi.**

Daniel.[9] Even so it points toward *Daniel* as does Buber's lengthy essay, "The Teaching of the Tao" (1910). In "The Teaching of the Tao," as in *Daniel,* the teaching means the realization of unity in genuine fulfilled life. This unity is no abstract conception, feeling, or act of will; no unity of world, knowledge, God, spirit, or being; rather, it is the unity of this human life and this human soul. Genuine life is united life. Fulfilling the teaching means lifting it out of the conditioned into the unconditioned, allowing all that is scattered, fleeting, and fragmentary to grow together to unity—a unity which is one's life. Human life itself is the bearer and reality of all transcendence. The perfect revelation of Tao is not the man who goes his way without change, but the man who combines the greatest change with the purest unity. The oneness of the world is only the reflection of the oneness of the perfect man, for the world is one with the united. It is in truth his unity which sets unity in the world. For though Tao is the path, order, and unity of everything, it exists in things only potentially until it becomes living and manifest through its contact with the conscious being of the united man. Tao appears in men as the uniting force that overcomes all deviation from the ground of life, as the completing force that heals all that is sundered and broken.[10]

In the preface to *Hinweise* (1953), the German collection in which the originals of all but seven of the essays in *Pointing the Way* appear, Buber writes that he has selected only essays that he can stand behind today. When I pointed out that this is not the case with "The Teach-

[9] **Buber,** Die Rede, die Lehre, und das Lied **(Leipzig: Insel Verlag, 1920), pp. 6 ff.**
[10] Pointing the Way, **pp. 45-58.**

ing of the Tao" since it affirms a mystical unity which *I and Thou* explicitly denies, he replied that it was necessary to include this essay because of its importance in the development of his thought and wrote a Foreword to *Pointing the Way* in which he states that "this small work belongs to a stage that I had to pass through before I could enter into an independent relationship with being." It is of the greatest importance that Buber's readers recognize that and why he had to pass through this stage and, at the same time, that he has definitely gone beyond it. The Taoist *wu-wei*—the action of the whole being that appears to be nonaction—still informs the second part of *I and Thou*. But the teaching of unity is no longer present in *I and Thou*. The experience of the unity of the self is understood by the mystic as the experience of *the* unity, and this leads him to turn away from his existence as a man to a duality of "higher" hours of ecstasy and "lower" hours in the world, which are regarded as preparation for the higher. "The great dialogue between I and Thou is silent; nothing else exists than his self, which he experiences as *the* self. That is certainly an exalted form of being untrue, but it is still being untrue." Buber sees the key to this inauthenticity in the fact that "instead of bringing into unity his whole existence as he lives it day by day, from the hours of blissful exaltation unto those of hardship and of sickness," the mystic "constantly flees from it into the experience of unity, into the detached feeling of unity of being, elevated above life." In doing this he "turns away from his existence as a man, the existence into which he has been set . . . for life and death in this unique personal form."[11]

[11] Ibid., **pp. xv ff.**

Daniel

While *Daniel* (1913) carries forward much of the teaching of the essential unity that is realized by the man who brings himself to unity, it attempts to move away from the unity of ecstasy above the world toward the unity of existence which is brought about through the inclusion of one's day-by-day life.

The German poet Rainer Maria Rilke had the same publisher (Insel Verlag) who published Buber's *Daniel*, and wrote with enthusiasm about *Daniel* when his publisher sent it to him.[12] According to the English scholar J. B. Morse, who wrote Martin Buber to this effect, Rilke was influenced by *Daniel* in writing his Ninth Duino Elegy. Much in the *Duino Elegies* suggests a kindred spirit between Rilke and the Buber of this period, and not a few passages in the Ninth Elegy make plausible Morse's suggestion of *Daniel*'s influence:

> *Why, when this span of life might be fleeted away*
> *as laurel, a little darker than all*
> *the surrounding green, with tiny waves on the border*
> *of every leaf (like the smile of a wind):—oh, why*
> have *to be human, and, shunning Destiny,*
> *long for Destiny? . . .*
>
> *Not because happiness really*
> *exists, that premature profit of imminent loss,*
> *Not out of curiosity, not just to practise the heart,*

[12] **Rilke,** Briefe am Seine Verleger **(Leipzig: Insel Verlag), pp. 180, 182. Buber has pointed out the affinity between** Daniel **and Rilke's** Book of Hours. **"We had to take similar paths," says Buber. "Any other leads into nihilism."**

that could still be there in laurel. . . . .
But because being here amounts to so much, because all
this Here and Now, so fleeting, seems to require us and strangely
concerns us. Us the most fleeting of all. Just once,
everything, only for once. Once and no more. And we, too,
once. And never again. But this
having been once, though only once,
having been once on earth—can it ever be cancelled?

And so we keep pressing on and trying to perform it,
trying to contain it within our simple hands,
in the more and more crowded gaze, in the speechless heart.
Trying to become it. To give it to whom? We'd rather
hold on to it all for ever. . . . Alas, but the other relation,—
what can be taken across? Not the art of seeing, learnt here
so slowly, and nothing that's happened here. Nothing at all.
Sufferings, then. Above all, the hardness of life,
the long experience of love; in fact,
purely untellable things. But later,
under the stars, what then? the more deeply untellable stars?
For the wanderer doesn't bring from the mountain slope
a handful of earth to the valley, untellable earth, but only
some word he has won, a pure word, the yellow and blue
gentian. Are we, perhaps, here just for saying: House,
Bridge, Fountain, Gate, Jug, Olive tree, Window,—
possibly: Pillar, Tower? . . . . but for saying, remember,
oh, for such saying as never the things themselves
hoped so intensely to be . . .

Here is the time for the Tellable, here is its home.
Speak and proclaim. More than ever
the things we can live with are falling away, and their place
being oustingly taken up by an imageless act.
Act under crusts, that will readily split as soon
as the doing within outgrows them and takes a new outline.
Between the hammers lives on
our heart, as between the teeth
the tongue, which, nevertheless,
remains the bestower of praise.

Praise the world to the Angel, not the untellable: you
can't impress him with the splendour you've felt; in the cosmos
where he more feelingly feels you're only a tyro. So show him
some simple thing, remoulded by age after age,
till it lives in our hands and eyes as a part of ourselves.
Tell him things. He'll stand more astonished; as you did
beside the roper in Rome or the potter in Egypt.
Show him how happy a thing can be, how guileless and ours;
how even the moaning of grief purely determines on form,
serves as a thing, or dies into a thing,—to escape
to a bliss beyond the fiddle. These things that live on departure
understand when you praise them: fleeting, they look for
rescue through something in us, the most fleeting of all.
Want us to change them entirely, within our invisible hearts,
into—oh, endlessly—into ourselves! Whosoever we are.[13]

[13] **Rainer Maria Rilke,** Duino Elegies, **trans. by J. B. Leishman and Stephen Spender (New York: W. W. Norton & Co., 1939), pp. 73, 75, 77.**

In *Daniel*, Buber's concern for unity, realization, creativity, action, and form is expressed for the first time entirely in its own terms and not as the interpretation of some particular thought or religious or cultural movement. *Daniel* is the first mature and comprehensive expression of Buber's early philosophy, and it is at the same time the most creative and organically whole of his books to appear until that time. It shows the way in which Buber's philosophy has grown out of a number of the decisive experiences of his life, and its poetic and dialogical form gives us an important emotional insight into Buber's early thought.

Each of *Daniel*'s five "Dialogues on Realization" takes its direction from a particular setting in which Daniel and one of his friends (a different one in each dialogue) happen to be together. In each of these dialogues Daniel is either the central figure or the one who states his views in response to a question or concern of his friend, and the concern of Daniel or his friend is in each case centered around one particular philosophical problem. Thus the dialogue in the mountains deals with direction, the dialogue above the city with reality, the dialogue in the garden with meaning, the dialogue after the theater with polarity, and the dialogue by the sea with unity.

Buber's concern with direction in the first dialogue presages his life-long emphasis upon combining passion and direction, the "evil" urge and the turning to God. It also presages Buber's important later doctrine of one's direction—one's unique path to God through which one fulfills the task to which one is called in one's creation. For Buber's earlier direction, as for the later, I discover the mystery waiting for me not as any form of predestination but through openness to

18

the seemingly chance, ever-new present that comes to meet me. Direction is only complete when it is fulfilled with power: the power to experience the whole event. Power alone gives one only the fullness, writes Buber in *Daniel,* direction alone, only the meaning of the experience—power and direction together allow one to penetrate into its substance, into oneness itself. Here, of course, is where Buber's early and his later uses of "direction" diverge; for in Buber's later thought direction never leads to unity but is an essential part of dialogue, which still includes an elemental experience of otherness.

In his 1912 essay "Das Gestaltende" ("The Formative") Buber posits a fundamental opposition between a formative and a formless principle, one that gives form and one that will not let itself be formed. Out of the opposition of these two principles the life of the spirit has again and again been born. This opposition is basically not between men but within each human soul, and the great conflict which takes place in history is only the projection into the life of the community of the conflict in the individual.[14] The "direction" of the first dialogue of *Daniel* is clearly related to the "form" of "Das Gestaltende" in that both direction and form stabilize and direct man's basic energies, thus making possible social living, cultural development, and personal integration and growth. Form, moreover, might properly be spoken of as a direction of energy. But direction does not threaten, like form, to bind man's life impulses so closely that they lose their vitality. Form becomes crystallized into external patterns that lose their connection with the life that produced them, thus distorting and suppressing energy rather than

[14] Die jüdische Bewegung, **I, 204-215.**

19

directing it. Direction, on the other hand, is like music. Music, says Daniel to the Woman, is the pure word of the directed soul which sets its inborn melody in the abyss, and the forces of the deep arrange themselves about it.

In *I and Thou* Buber characterizes all types of experience as I-It. Experiencing is I-It whether it is the experiencing of an object or of a man, whether it is "inner" or "outer," "open" or "secret." One's life of interior feeling is in no way elevated above one's life with the external world, nor is the occultist's knowledge of secret mysteries anything but the inclusion of the unseen in the world of It. The reason for Buber's refusal to join his contemporaries in an unqualified affirmation of "experience" is the typically modern tendency to invert the original meaning of the term. Instead of going out to an experience, we "have" an experience. Whatever it is that we encounter thus becomes a content of our soul that we have robbed of its real otherness. In *Daniel* Buber's concern for preserving the otherness of the other as Thou has not fully matured. But Buber is concerned about the uniqueness of what one meets and about the difference between a merely external, manipulative relationship to it and one that one enters with one's whole being. To express this concern he distinguishes in the first dialogue of *Daniel* and in all those that follow between *Erfahrung* (the word for experience in the German original of *I and Thou*) and *Erlebnis*. If *Erlebnis* is not yet I-Thou, it is also not I-It; for it demands a personal participation and involvement that I-It does not demand. I have translated *Erlebnis* throughout as "life-experience" to distinguish it from the more mechanical and external experience which Buber consigns to the world of It in *I and Thou*.

20

The distinction in the first dialogue between the man who protects himself from the chaos of experience through causality and order and the man who goes out to meet it with the strength of his inborn direction is given further and fuller development in the second dialogue, "On Reality," and the third, "On Meaning." In the dialogue on direction no limits were suggested to the individual's power to live by direction nor was it suggested that a man's direction could become, like social and cultural forms, something external and rigid. In the dialogue on reality, however, it is recognized that the individual cannot, any more than the community, always live in direct contact with reality. Thus the alternation that Buber describes in "Zwiefache Zukunft" ("Twofold Future of the Jewish Movement," 1912) between the direct experience of life through religious renewal and the cultural forms which at first express and later distort that experience[15] is reproduced here in the life of the individual, for whom hours of orientation must follow hours of realization. In this respect *Daniel* forms a clear transition to the alternation between the I-Thou relationship and the I-It relation that lies at the heart of *I and Thou*.

To realize means to relate experience to nothing else but itself, says Daniel. Here is the place where the strength of the human spirit awakens and concentrates and becomes creative. Whereas in orienting, one has only to arrange and order, and living with only one part of one's being can come to terms with the all, in realizing, one must bring forth the totality of one's being in order to withstand a single thing or event. That alone is true reality which is so experienced. As

[15] **Cf. Maurice Friedman,** Martin Buber: The Life of Dialogue, **p. 40.**

in the life of the community, attained reality must ever again be placed in the continuity of experience; so in the life of the individual, hours of orienting follow hours of realizing and must so follow. But the creative man is he who has the most effective power of realization; he is the man in whom the realizing force of the soul has so concentrated into work that it creates reality for all. The creative man possesses the unbroken power of realization, for in his creativity mature orientation is included as a dependent and serving function. Realized experience creates the essential form of existence; only here can what we call "things" and what we call "I" find their reality.

The fact that each man has both the power and the responsibility to realize, and that this realization can penetrate even the hours of orientation, shows that Buber's philosophy of realization does not mean a lofty divorce from the limitations of existence but a real progress in bringing the stubborn stuff of life into the circle of lived and meaningful experience. In our age, however, this task is far more difficult than before, for in our age orientation predominates as at no earlier time. Although the domination of orientation is linked with the progress of science and of "objective information" about the world, this progress is not repudiated as evil in itself. What is evil is that the thousand petty means of life have each of them taken on the features of ends in themselves so that man no longer has a true goal but is ruled by his instruments. Human life, as a result, becomes impersonal, mediate, and instrumental, and realization is replaced by appearance and imitation. "Realizing men are few in our age" which "is busy replacing them by the producers . . . who work without being, who give what they do not possess, who triumph where they have not fought." This thought is expanded by Buber in one of his

22

most important and still relevant early essays, "Productivity and Existence":

> The overvaluation of productivity that is afflicting our age has so thrived and its pan-technical glance has set up so senseless an exclusiveness of its own that even genuinely creative men allow their organic skills to degenerate . . . to satisfy the demand of the day. What the born deceivers never had, they give up: the ground where the roots of a genuine lived life alone can grow. . . . They wear themselves out turning all experience to account as public communication; they renounce true necessity and give themselves over to the arbitrary. They poison experience, for already while it is taking place they are dominated by the will to produce. . . . They forfeit both life and art, and all that they gain is the applause of their production-mad contemporaries. . . . He who meets men with a double glance, an open one that invites his fellows to sincerity and the concealed one of the observer stemming from a conscious aim; he who in friendship and in love is cleft into two men, one who surrenders himself to his feelings and another who is already standing by to exploit them—this man cannot be delivered by any creative talent from the blight that he has brought upon himself and his work, for he has poisoned the springs of his life.[16]

It may be objected that the vagueness of Buber's philosophy of realization detracts from its value and meaning. This objection is in part well founded, for there is much in *Daniel* that is beclouded with aesthetic language and a very special and subjective mystical emo-

[16] Pointing the Way, **pp. 8-10.**

tion. This fact is brought out particularly clearly by comparing *Daniel* with *I and Thou,* in which many of the same concepts are expressed in much clearer form and illustrated in terms of much more universal experience, while the language has gained in beauty and force. But the lack of clarity in *Daniel* must in part be explained by the fact that its concepts remain close to direct experience and therefore cannot be neatly ordered in the world of orientation, in which human experience is dealt with only after it has first been abstracted.

The third dialogue, "On Meaning. Dialogue in the Garden," centers on Daniel's friend Reinold who tells him of the happy years of his childhood and young manhood when the meaning of life seemed assured of itself and even his troubles and conflicts seemed a trusted part of him. Reinold's descriptions of his childhood as "the land with the living heart . . . golden rimmed with meaning" and of the later time when all that was trusted seemed strange and hostile are reminiscent both in style and thought of Dylan Thomas' classic poem "Fern Hill":

> *Now as I was young and easy under the apple boughs*
> *About the lilting house and happy as the grass was green,*
> > *The night above the dingle starry,*
> > > *Time let me hail and climb*
> > *Golden in the heydays of his eyes,*
> *And honored among wagons I was prince of the apple towns*
> *And once below a time I lordly had the trees and leaves*
> > > *Trail with daisies and barley*
> > *Down the rivers of the windfall light.*

And honored among foxes and pheasants by the gay house
Under the new-made clouds and happy as the heart was long
   In the sun born over and over,
       I ran my heedless ways,
     My wishes raced through the house-high hay
And nothing I cared, at my sky blue trades, that time allows
In all his tuneful turning so few and such morning songs
     Before the children green and golden
         Follow him out of grace.

.   .   .   .

And wake to the farm forever fled from the childless land.
Oh as I was young and easy in the mercy of his means,
     Time held me green and dying
     Though I sang in my chains like the sea.

Reinold's experience of the abyss is a clear continuation of many motifs in Buber's earlier thought—the individual's hopeless solitude and eternal distance from the world, the schism between thought and action, life and spirit, the abysses of being which the creative man must face, and the universal inner duality of man. The most striking prototype of Reinold's abyss is a passage from "The Revelation," one of Buber's early legends of the Baal-Shem:

The world lay before him like an abyss. Out of the abyss emerged the solar disk in silent torment. In agonized birth pangs the earth brought forth trees and plants without number, and many animals ran and flew in senseless motion. Each creature suffered because it must do what it did, could not get free, and gasped in its pain. All things were enveloped by the abyss, and yet the whole abyss was between each thing and the other. None could cross over to the other, indeed none could see the other, for the abyss was between them.[17]

Reinold tells Daniel of his efforts to find security and of his dissatisfaction with all the theologians, philosophers, and scientists with their ready-made formulas, none of which touched his inner experience. The clarity and force of Daniel's response is a testimony to the development of Buber's thought beyond the first two dialogues, and the directness of the style makes impossible the criticism of aestheticism and preciousness that might be leveled against earlier passages. All living with the whole being and with unconstrained force means danger, says Daniel; there is no thing, relation, or event in the world that does not reveal an abyss when it is known, and all thinking threatens to shatter the stability of the thinker. He who lives his life in genuine, realizing knowledge must perpetually begin anew, perpetually risk all; and therefore his truth is not a having but a becoming. The orienting man wants security once for all: he wants a solid general truth that will not overturn him. God cannot realize himself in men otherwise than as the innermost presence of an experience, and the God of this experience is therefore not the same, but always the new, the uttermost. Orientation which acts as the all-embracing is thoroughly godless, says Daniel, in presage of Buber's later attack on that theology which turns God into an It and that gnosis which schematizes the mystery.

The realizing man has that before which all security appears vain and

[17] **Martin Buber,** The Legend of the Baal-Shem, **trans. by Maurice Friedman (New York: Harper & Row, 1955), pp. 69 ff.**

empty: direction and meaning. The deed is not limited for him, as it is for the orienting man, to causality and evolution; he feels himself free and acts as a free man—a statement which Buber later makes of the man who lives in the I-Thou relationship as opposed to the I-It. The orienting man places all happening in formulas, rules, and connections; the realizing man relates each event to nothing but its own intrinsic value and exactly thereby makes of it a sign of the eternal. Here Buber anticipates not only the relation with the Eternal Thou which is found in the temporal Thou—in the present and the unique —but also his later definition of religion as the covenant of the Absolute with the particular, as revelation in the "lived concrete."

He who has meaning and direction celebrates in his living a new mystery: the experience of realizing God in all things. For God wills to be realized, and all reality is God's reality, and there is no reality except through men who realize themselves and all being. This is the kingdom of God: the kingdom of danger and of risk, of eternal beginning and of eternal becoming, of revealed spirit and of deep realization, the kingdom of "holy insecurity." Danger is the door of deep reality, and reality is the highest prize of life and the eternal birth of God. He who descends into the transforming abyss can create unity out of his and out of all duality. Here no "once-for-all" is of value; for this is the endless task.

This doctrine of God's becoming through man's realization of him in all things is closer to the later works of Rilke and even of Martin Heidegger ("Man is the shepherd of Being") than to Buber's own mature thought. Of his equation of the kingdom of God with "holy insecurity" Buber wrote me forty years later: "Today I would not any more describe the kingdom so extravagantly!"[18] Yet the emphasis on "holy insecurity" remains central in Buber's thought from this time on. In an address to the dogmatists of the law, written in 1919, Buber says:

> *O you secure and safe ones who hide yourselves behind the defense-works of the law so that you will not have to look into God's abyss! Yes, you have secure ground under your feet while we hang suspended, looking out over the endless deeps. But we would not exchange our dizzy insecurity and our poverty for your security and abundance. . . . To you God is one who revealed himself once and no more; but to us he speaks out of the burning thorn-bush of the present . . . in the revelations of our innermost hearts—greater than words.*[19]

"Holy insecurity" also lies behind Buber's contrast between *gnosis* and *devotio*, between the Kabbala and Hasidism:

> *The whole systematic structure of the Kabbala is determined by the principle of a certitude that almost never stops short, almost never shudders, almost never prostrates itself. In contrast it is just in stopping short, in letting itself be disconcerted, in deep knowledge of the impotence of all "information," of the incongruence of all possessed truth, in the "holy insecurity," that Hasidic piety has its true life.*[20]

"Holy insecurity" is also central to Buber's understanding of the

[18] From a letter of Martin Buber to Maurice Friedman, August 8, 1954.

[19] **Martin Buber,** Reden über das Judentum (Frankfurt am Main: Rütten & Loening, 1923), "Der Heilige Weg," pp. 65, 71 (my translation).

[20] **Buber,** The Origin and Meaning of Hasidism, **ed. & trans. with an Introduction by Maurice Friedman (New York: Horizon Press, 1960), p. 179.**

genuine Hebrew prophet who, in contrast to the apocalyptic, calls man to real decision and response in openness in the historical hour. The prophets of Israel, writes Buber in reproof of Heidegger, "always aimed to shatter all security and to proclaim in the opened abyss of the final insecurity the unwished-for God who demands that His human creatures become real . . . and confounds all who imagine that they can take refuge in the certainty that the temple of God is in their midst."[21] Closely similar is Buber's contrast between *pistis,* faith in a proposition by which Buber characterizes the faith of Paul and John, and *emuna,* the unconditional trust in the grace which Buber sees as central not only to the Hebrew Bible but also to the teachings of Jesus. The number of Christian images that appear in *Daniel* should not mislead the reader. Buber has been concerned about Jesus from his early writings, but he sees Jesus not as a Christian but as a Jew.

The man of realization is not unlike the perfected man of "The Teaching of the Tao" who purifies the world through purifying himself, who is helpful to others through collecting himself, and who renews creation through true action, or "nonaction," the working of the whole being. But he can also be identified with Buber's 1908 image of the Hasid, for whom the character of the action is determined not by its nature but by its dedication and who is at home in the world without any special protection:

> He knows that all is in God and greets His messengers as trusted friends. He has no fear of the before and the after, of the above and the

[21] **Buber,** Eclipse of God. Studies in the Relation of Religion to Philosophy, **trans. by Maurice Friedman,** et al. (**New York: Harper Torchbooks, 1957), p. 73.**

below, of this world and the world to come. He is at home and never can be cast out. The earth cannot help but be his cradle, and heaven cannot help but be his mirror and his echo.[22]

Those who are familiar with Kierkegaard's category of *Angst* will of course think of him in connection with Buber's "holy insecurity," particularly of Kierkegaard's "knight of faith" in *Fear and Trembling* who lives in danger and must constantly risk all:

> *The knight of faith knows . . . that it is beautiful and salutary to be the individual who translates himself into the universal, who edits as it were a pure and elegant edition of himself, as free from errors as possible and which every one can read. . . . But he knows also that higher than this there winds a solitary path, narrow and steep; he knows that it is terrible to be born outside the universal, to walk without meeting a single traveler. . . . The knight of faith knows that to give up oneself for the universal inspires enthusiasm, and that it requires courage, but he also knows that security is to be found in this precisely because it is for the universal. . . . The hero does the deed and finds repose in the universal, the knight of faith is kept in constant tension.*[23]

The tension of the knight of faith, however, is the tension between the finite, which he renounces and yet hopes to regain through faith "by virtue of the absurd," and the infinite for which he renounces it; while the tension of the man of realization is that of the immanent

[22] The Legend of the Baal-Shem, **p. 50.**

[23] **Søren Kierkegaard,** Fear and Trembling, **trans. by Walter Lowrie (New York: Anchor Books, 1954), p. 86.**

30

duality of all things and in the depths of his being—the abyss into which he must descend to bring unity to himself and to the world.

It is this duality which is the subject of the fourth dialogue, "On Polarity. Dialogue After the Theater." What I saw in the play, says Daniel, was the spectacle of duality. But not good and evil: all valuation was only external dress; rather the primal duality itself, being and counterbeing, opposed to one another and bound to one another as pole with pole—the free polarity of the human spirit. This polarity anticipates Buber's later philosophy of the relation between "I" and "Thou" which can never become a union. Daniel sees this polarity in the opposition of audience and actors, of actor and actor, and of the great actor and the hero whom he represents not through weakening the opposition and becoming one with him but through preserving the polar tension and yet transforming himself in him. It is interesting to note how important a part drama has played in the development of Buber's philosophy of dialogue. In 1905 in a discussion of the great actress Eleonora Duse, Buber used the term "I and Thou" to characterize the drama and the tension of the isolated individual.[24] In 1913 Buber took his view of the theater further in "The Space Problem of the Stage," written for experiments in the Hellerau theater in which he participated and which he advised. And in 1925 he developed a complete theory of dialogue in "Drama and the Theater." It is easy to see from this essay how Buber's teaching of polarity in the drama in *Daniel* flowered into dialogue, tension, the between, the word, and the I-Thou relationship as the center of both drama as poetry and drama as theater. "Regarded as a

[24] Buber, "Die Duse in Florenz," Die Schaubühne, Vol. I, No. 15 (December 14, 1905).

species of poetry," writes Buber, "drama is . . . the formation of the *word* as something that moves *between beings,* the mystery of word and answer. Essential to it is the fact of the *tension* between word and answer; the fact, namely, that two men never mean the same things by the words that they use; . . . from which comes then the interplay of openness and closedness, expression and reserve." Thus dramatic entanglement already exists through the mere fact of the *difference* between men, and this fact is given form by dialogue. It is to the command of this *word,* mixture of understanding and misunderstanding, that the theater must submit: ". . . The stern over-againstness of I and Thou, overarched by the wonder of speech, that governs all the play of transformation, weaving the mystery of the spirit into every element—it alone can determine the legitimate relation between drama and theater."[25]

It is not surprising, therefore, that despite the emphasis on unity in so much of the rest of *Daniel,* the dialogue after the theater should single out polarity and anticipate the "over-againstness," the ever-renewed distancing that precedes relationship in both Buber's I-Thou philosophy and his later philosophical anthropology. Here is the root too of Buber's distinction in his mature philosophy between "empathy" and "inclusion." In his 1901 essay on Boehme he rejected the "over-against" as the separation of subject and object. Now he accepts it as essential to the otherness and concrete uniqueness of the Thou. This concrete uniqueness is apprehended in an action that Buber variously calls "imagining the real," "experiencing the other side of the relation," and "inclusion," and it is in this

[25] Pointing the Way, **pp. 63-66. "The Space Problem of the Stage" is also included in** Pointing the Way.

32

fourth dialogue of *Daniel,* in connection with the theater and the great play, that he first uses the term "inclusion" (*Umfassung*) in this significant sense.

"Experiencing the other side" means to feel an event from the side of the person one meets as well as from one's own side. It is an inclusiveness which realizes the other person in the actuality of his being, but it must not be identified with "empathy," which means transposing oneself into the dynamic structure of an object, hence, "the exclusion of one's own concreteness, the extinguishing of the actual situation of life, the absorption in pure aestheticism of the reality in which one participates." Inclusion is the opposite of this. "It is the extension of one's own concreteness, the fulfillment of the actual situation of life, the complete presence of the reality in which one participates." In inclusion one person, "without forfeiting anything of the felt reality of his activity, at the same time lives through the common event from the standpoint of the other."[26]

From the pure polarity of the theater Daniel proceeds to the more broken and imperfect polarity of human life. But in human life, as in drama, all high excitement has its origin in a polarity which is to be lived, realized, carried out. Polarity may be reached through the decision of the man who fights for unity, through inclusion—the love in which a genuinely present man embraces being—, or through the knowledge in which the man who cannot perceive or ascertain the mystery of the world penetrates it through transformation. The secret of the world is the binding of meaning and being, not through reflection but through realization—the imitation of the unknown

[26] **Buber,** Between Man and Man, **"Education," pp. 96 ff.**

God. It is this imitation which Buber points to in "Education" (1925) as the ultimate goal of the modern educator.

All action of men is creation and destruction combined, and each acting man must, knowingly or unknowingly, reject the much that might arise through him for the sake of the one thing that he chooses. As this rejection is the indispensable prelude to the creation of form, so it is also the prerequisite of constructive living. If there were a devil, says Buber in *I and Thou,* "it would not be one who decided against God, but one who in eternity came to no decision." This is the man who leaves himself in "the menace of the abyss, the center-less Many" which "plays in the iridescent sameness of its pretensions."[27]

Evil then does not lie in one part of the polarity as against the other nor in the polarity itself. It lies in the attempt to weaken the tension of the polarity and in the failure to fulfill it and bring it to unity. If out of this unity new polarity arises, so also new polarity provides the occasion for the creation of new unity. The creation of this unity which never is, but only becomes, is the task of man.

In this fourth dialogue one finds the fruit of Buber's meditations on form and formlessness and decayed form in "The Formative" (1912) and his progress in "Twofold Future of the Jewish Movement" (1912) to the recognition that religion is not form but the renewal of the life impulses and life forms between two cultural develop-

[27] **Martin Buber,** I and Thou, **2nd revised edition with Postscript by author added, trans. by Ronald Gregor Smith (New York: Charles Scribner's Sons, 1958, Scribner's Paperback, 1960), p. 52.**

ments. While formlessness was previously almost a positive evil, in "Twofold Future" Buber puts forward a dialectical polarity in which he sees an alternation between the forms of culture and the "fruitful chaos" of religion. Religion becomes the revolutionary principle which destroys old forms and releases suppressed power. Thus the new form that arises, like the decision of the acting man in *Daniel*, is creation and destruction combined. In the life of a people as in the life of an individual what is important is the polar duality, neither pole of which is evil: "Power of the storming spirit to stir up the conflagration, security of the constructing soul to hold itself in the purifying fire: these are the forces which guide a people to rejuvenated life."[28]

In the fifth dialogue of *Daniel*, Buber sets forth his most mature conclusions up to this time on the problem of unity. This dialogue is the most moving and profound of all the dialogues and is in a very real sense the culmination of the other four. It is entitled "On Unity. Dialogue by the Sea," yet its most important emotional focus is on death and the relation between death and life. It is interesting to note how often the sea has entered into these dialogues, how often it has been a symbol of an incomprehensible infinity that threatens man's existence or a motherly infinite with which man desires to become one. In the first dialogue, "On Direction," Buber does not stop with the experience of the sea as a hostile infinity, as does Melville in *Moby Dick*. He goes on to make of it an opponent who is no longer terrifying and hostile as soon as one has chosen one's own direction from the countless possibilities that lie open to one. In the third dialogue, "On Meaning," Reinold tells Daniel of how the childhood

[28] Die jüdische Bewegung, **I, 216-220.**

security which he had retained even into manhood was lost one day when he went out on the sea in a small boat and the pleasant lapping of the water was suddenly transformed into horror. In the fifth dialogue, "On Unity," the conversation actually takes place by the sea. Lukas shows Daniel the place where a mutual friend one year before sailed out to sea and fell or stepped from his boat and was drowned. Lukas feels as if he sets sail every morning in the boat of his dead friend in which the demon of life sits at the rudder and the goddess of death in the prow. From day to day the question mounts in him: What sort of a sea is it on which we voyage, what sort of a sea is it that has given birth to us, what is the holy sea that bears life and death in right and left hand? In a figure strikingly similar to one that Meursault uses in Camus' novel *The Stranger,* he speaks of the strange wind that is blowing backward toward him from his future death in contrast to time—the force of life that bears him onward.

He who genuinely experiences the world, Daniel tells Lukas, experiences it as duality. Out of the play of the manifold he brings forth the essential line of tension. And to overcome this tension is his task. Duality is many-named and multiform, but it remains the same in the tension. All wisdom of the ages has the duality of the world as its subject, the union of their duality as its goal. But the true man will not surrender anything of the fullness of his experience because of his longing for unity: he preserves his experienced duality undiminished in the force of its distance. For this reason he rejects the Absolute of the Vedantic nondualists as a life-denying unity apart from the highroad on which the faithful man must travel. He rejects in like manner the abstract unity of European idealist philosophy and the empty unity of the Taoist who makes all opposites indifferent in himself. True unity is a unity which excludes nothing and destroys nothing, but transforms the stubborn material of life into oneness through the realizing action of men. It is the unity which includes all evil, for it can accept nothing less than the whole, but just for this reason it is never completely attained but comes forth ever again as purer and sharper duality. Each new act of inner unification enables the individual to take to himself ever greater tensions of world-polarity and bring them to unity. Thus, this fifth dialogue is a continuation rather than a rejection of the polarity of the fourth.

It is here that Buber makes clear why he had to go through mysticism to reach his independent relationship to the truth. Each of the three wrong ways produced truth in the faithful one, says Daniel, each ripened a layer of the teaching to conscious being. They confirmed in him the striving for unity: what he beheld detached guaranteed him fulfillment; what yielded itself to him in the formless depths knows also how to rise to him out of the world of form; what revealed itself to him in self-collection must prove true in the scattered totality of his experience. It is possible for us to trace the development of Buber's thought from mysticism to dialogue even more explicitly than this, however, through an experience which Daniel tells Lukas. One morning walking upon the highway, he was attracted by a piece of mica. After looking at it he realized that in his looking the stone and the "I" had been one—he had experienced unity. The unity did not return when he looked again but only when, closing his eyes, he bound himself with his object and raised the stone into the kingdom of being. The first unity was non-differentiation, but the second was unification, and only with the second came the feeling "I."

In "Ecstasy and Confession" (1909) Buber speaks of the grace of unity which may be kindled through looking at a heap of stones. One is no longer aware of looking at a rock, one experiences only unity, the world: oneself. All forces are united and felt as unity, and in the middle of them lives and shines the stone which is contemplated. The soul experiences the unity of the "I," and in it the unity of "I" and the world, no longer a content but that which is infinitely more than all content.[29] This is the unity realized apart from the world, the unity of the nondualist mystic which Daniel has described as one of the wrong ways from which the faithful man has turned. Commenting on the same experience of looking at a stone (very possibly the identical experience in Buber's life), Daniel says to Lukas: True unity cannot be found, it can only be created. He who creates it realizes the unity of the world in the unity of his soul. Thus he must previously experience the tension of the world as his own soul's tension. This contrast makes all the more significant the fact we have already noted, namely, that in the introduction to *Die Rede, die Lehre, und das Lied* (1920), Buber explicitly rejected his treatment of unity in "Ecstasy and Confession" for that of the fifth dialogue of *Daniel*.

This does not mean that Buber has rejected the experience of looking at the mica itself. Rather he has reinterpreted his earlier mystical experience in the light of later experience and thought. This fact casts light on the limitations of any one experience, even a mystic experience, in providing a permanently valid knowledge. But it also shows how all previous experience may enter into and remain the material for a growth in wisdom that rejects no earlier stage yet

[29] Ekstatische Konfessionen, **p. xii.**

remains frozen at no one formulation. It is not, as Buber puts it in this dialogue, that one experience simply joins itself to another and thereby reveals the truth of the first, for our interpretation of each successive experience is a dialogue with it that enters into the truth we receive from it. Thus in *I and Thou* (1923) and "Dialogue" (1929) Buber does not reject the unity of the soul which the mystic experiences, yet he no longer interprets it as union with primal being, the godhead, or the world, but as the undifferentiated unity of the soul itself. In the same way in *I and Thou* the experience of looking at the mica is taken up, not to give it a new interpretation, indeed, but to recognize that the knowledge gained from the experience was limited:

> *O fragment of mica, looking on which I once learned, for the first time, that* I *is not something "in me"—with you I was nevertheless only bound up in myself; at that time the event took place only in me, not between me and you.*[30]

Thus the experience itself stayed with Buber as a hidden store of potential knowledge, not simply reinterpreted but ever more deeply understood in the light of new experience. It is only through the recognition of the role which this interrelation of experiences plays in the constructions of a philosophy of a life that we can see the meaning and value of an experience-based philosophy such as Buber's.

At one point Daniel speaks to Lukas of how "the final level of the teaching" ripened in him. How far this teaching of the fifth dialogue

[30] I and Thou, **p. 98.**

of *Daniel* is from being final! Yet how seminal *Daniel* is for Buber's later thought! There is no stress in *Daniel* on the "interhuman"—the dialogue between man and man which occupies so much of Buber's later attention. Yet if we recall that the I-Thou relationship for Buber is not confined to the interhuman but also includes nature and art, we can see how clearly the relational and polar character of the fifth dialogue of *Daniel* anticipates *I and Thou*: "There is in reality no I except the I of a tension: in which it brings itself together," says Daniel. "No pole, no force, no thing—only polarity, only stream, only unification can become I."

In *Daniel*, the mystic's demand for a life lived in terms of the highest reality and the existentialist's demand for self-realization and genuine existence meet in spirit and produce a new, if not a final, teaching—the philosophy of realization.

From Realization to Dialogue

If *Daniel* so clearly anticipates Buber's I-Thou philosophy, we must ask why Professor Buber wrote me that it expresses the great duality of human life "only in its cognitive and not yet in its communicative and existential character." This question can best be answered through a comparison between *Daniel* and the essay which more than any other stands as the transitional stage between *Daniel* and *I and Thou*—"With a Monist." In "With a Monist" we find again the realizing man of *Daniel*, the man who sees reality not as a fixed condition but as a greatness which can be enhanced, the man who does not want to remove the world of the senses but to intensify it, the man who establishes unity in the world out of experienced unity, "for unity is not a property of the world but its task."

Now, however, the two aspects of life—the orienting and the realizing—no longer apply merely to man himself and are no longer simply epistemological—a way of knowing. They apply rather to what is over against man and his relation to what meets him, and they are ontological—the reality *between* man and the things.

> *Each thing and being has a twofold nature: the passive, absorbable, usable, dissectible, comparable, combinable, rationalizable, and the other, the active, non-absorbable, unusable, undissectible, incomparable, noncombinable, nonrationalizable. This is the confronting, the shaping, the bestowing in things. He who truly experiences a thing so that it springs up to meet him of itself has in that thing known the world.*

I give reality to my world "by bending over the experienced thing with fervor and with power and by melting the shell of passivity with the fire of my being until the confronting, the shaping, the bestowing side of things springs up to meet me and embraces me."[31]

Thus in two essential respects, "With a Monist" forms a transition between *Daniel* and *I and Thou*. For in his I-Thou philosophy Buber also posits the twofold nature of things as qualities not only of knowledge but of being. And in *I and Thou*, as in "With a Monist," the emphasis is not so much on the unity of things, not even the realized unity of *Daniel*, but on the meeting between man and what is over against him, a meeting which becomes a relationship but never an identity. Here is the root of that uniqueness which stands at the center of the I-Thou relationship and here is the key to Buber's

[31] Pointing the Way, **pp. 27-30.**

I-Thou relationship with nature in which the existing beings over against us move to meet us as we them. Although we cannot isolate and objectify this impact, we know it in the relation in the present moment between our human "I" and that nonhuman existing being which has become real for us as "Thou." This impact makes manifest the only true uniqueness, that which comes from relating to a thing in itself and not in terms of its comparison with other things and its ordering into categories.

Being and Becoming

In 1923, in the Foreword to his collected "Talks on Judaism," Buber made several explicit corrections of his earlier teachings in the light of the new insight of *I and Thou*. Some of these corrections clearly apply to *Daniel*. God does not arise out of the striving for unity, Buber now says, only the image of God, the idea of God, and even this arises not out of the human but out of the meeting of the divine and the human. The meeting with God is no myth-projecting fantasy. It arises not out of "experience" and detached subjectivity, but out of life. The concept of the realization of God is not inexact or improper in itself, writes Buber, but it is improperly applied when one speaks of making God out of a truth into a reality. It can thus mislead one to the opinion that God is an "idea" which becomes "reality" only through men, and further to the hopelessly perverted conception that God is not, but rather becomes—in man or in mankind. This opinion is perverted not because there is no divine becoming in the immanence, but because only through the primal certainty of divine being can we come into contact with the mysterious meaning of divine becoming, the self-division of God in creation and his participation in the destiny of its freedom.

By the same token the summons of our human existence cannot be to overcome the division of being and reality in order to let the divine take seed, grow, and ripen in the perceptible world. We cannot hold with the concept of a reality which is relative and far from God. This concept comes from a division between the "thinking" and the "feeling" relation of the "subject" and makes of this psychological and relative duality of functions an absolute duality of spheres. If we comprehend ourselves in the God-world fullness in which we live, then we recognize that "to realize God" means to make the world ready to be a place of God's reality.[32]

Henceforth, the emphasis in Buber's thought is not, as heretofore, on the process of realization but on the meeting of God and man and the theophany that illuminates human life and history as the result of that meeting. Only in this development has Buber gone decisively beyond the subjectivistic and time-centered vitalism of Nietzsche and Bergson. Only through this final step has he reached the understanding that, though the external form changes, the essence of theophany—the meeting between man and God—remains the same. "God wills to ripen in men," Buber has written; yet it is not God himself who changes and ripens but the depth and fullness of man's encounter with God and the ways in which man expresses this meeting and makes it meaningful for his daily life. Buber's shift in emphasis to the reciprocal meeting of God and man leaves no further room for the concept of an impersonal godhead coming to birth in the soul. God is now, to Buber, the Eternal Thou, the Absolute Person, "nearer to me than my I," yet revealing himself in my meeting with the Other.

[32] Reden über das Judentum, **pp. xi ff.**

You know always in your heart that you need God more than every-thing; but do you not know too that God needs you—in the fullness of His eternity needs you? . . . You need God, in order to be—and God needs you, for the very meaning of your life. In instruction and in poems men are at pains to say more, and they say too much—what turgid and presumptuous talk that is about the "God who becomes"; but we know unshakeably in our hearts that there is a becoming of the God that is. . . . We take part in creation, meet the Creator, reach out to Him, helpers and companions.[33]

Buber speaks in *I and Thou* of a double movement "of estrangement from the primal Source, in virtue of which the universe is sustained in the process of becoming, and of turning toward the primal Source, in virtue of which the universe is released in being." This is the "becoming of the God that is." Both parts of the movement develop, "fraught with destiny in time, and are compassed by grace in the timeless creation that is, incomprehensibly, at once emancipa-tion and preservation, release and binding." More than this on being and becoming, Buber will not say: "Our knowledge of twofold nature is silent before the paradox of the primal mystery."[34]

[33] I and Thou, **p. 82.**
[34] Ibid., **p. 101.**

Author's Preface

*After a descent during which I had to utilize without a halt the late light
of a dying day, I stood on the edge of a meadow, now sure of the safe way,
and let the twilight come down upon me. Not needing a support and
yet willing to accord my lingering a fixed point, I pressed my stick
against a trunk of an oak tree. Then I felt in twofold fashion my contact
with being: here, where I held the stick, and there, where it touched
the bark. Appearing to be only where I was, I nonetheless found myself
there, too, where I found the tree.*

*At that time dialogue appeared to me. For the speech of man, wherever
it is genuine speech, is like that stick; that means: truly directed
address. Here, where I am, where ganglia and organs of speech help me
to form and to send forth the word, here I "mean" him to whom I send it,
I intend him, this one unexchangeable man. But also there, where he is,
something of me is delegated, something that is not at all substantial
in nature like that being-here, rather pure vibration and incomprehensible;
that remains there, with him, the man meant by me, and takes part in
the receiving of my word. I encompass him to whom I turn.*

I On Direction. Dialogue in the Mountains

Daniel: Let us go further. I take no pleasure in resting in the midst of the mountains. One must be able to remain upright, uphill, downhill, until one again stands in the valley and in the usual order. If we sit down up here, we shall have established the mastery of the plains in this place to which it should never reach. To me it is as if we injured the meaning of things. I am ashamed of my body which cannot preserve its steepness until it is achieved. The rocks tower in the air like a call, like an accusation. And only then do they become my brothers.

The Woman: But in rising do you not feel all the more precipitously the revelation that it is granted you to climb? Are not the hollows of your knees made threefold happy to be permitted again to stretch? Again—that is the great jubilation of our lives.

Would we not be miserable—creatures flung into a stale existence—
if we were not born again every morning out of the abyss of sleep?

Daniel: Yes, that is the breath of the earth, the indispensable.
Because we cannot breathe like eternal beings who exhale the one,
directionless world-breath, we make for ourselves out of the
game of in and out a small sensual delight. Because we cannot
circle above all existence—sleepless, unbroken, boundless,
glowing—we content ourselves with being submerged and
awakening. Because we cannot ascend into the spaceless . . .

The Woman: Into the spaceless?

Daniel: Into the spaceless! For it is that, indeed, that lifts and
blesses us for climbing: that we liberate ourselves from the prison
of direction-building. *Seem* to liberate ourselves, you may say.
But I cannot measure my life-experience by a more valid reality
when it has been for me the most valid of all. I still know how
it happened to me the first time. What happened? A crossbeam
detached itself from the cross of the space to which I was bound,
and soon my feet were also free: I stood up free in the vertical,
and I was the vertical. For only now did I feel in truth the meaning
of my upright body, my upright body-soul. I lifted my arms
above my head in order to intensify still further this uprightness,
and soon the flames beat upward from my heels to my fingernails,
and no cathedral's buttress ever stood with such extended life as I.

The Woman: I sense it, Daniel, what you say, and as something
slumbering, dreaming in me. But how can you think of this

triumph of penetrating space as an ascent into the spaceless?

Daniel: Is not space the clearest form of the great occurrence in which the One is intersected by the Many? And is not this, our way, a passionate image of that free enduring in the One that is denied us?

Certainly, what I experienced as I stood uplifted between heaven and earth was still space and had to remain such; but reflected therein was a kingdom in which there is nothing except my self and over it its completion. For no breadth was there that intersected my uplifting. The torch of my tension burnt unflickering to the zenith; undiverted, the lightning of the heights hurled down on my head, and earthly fire mixed itself with heavenly fire. The scaffolding of directions had caved in; I, the one set upright, was alone with my direction. And at that time the grace appeared to me which makes one who is borne into one who bears.

For what is it that we feel ourselves surrendered to since the might of our life is still confirmed with immortal seals? . . . Do you still know that evening over the sea?

The Woman: Our room hung over the sea. The shore could not be seen. When one looked out, one stood over the water, yes, one stood in the air over the water like a sea gull in turning, like a spirit which hovering pauses and looks. I leaned on the open window in the evening . . .

Daniel: You leaned on the open window in the evening; the small waves of the sea played against you, and you felt the small waves of your blood in unison with them, felt a mild melancholy and all security. Then you took your eyes away for a moment, you lowered them again half involuntarily, then the world was transformed: instead of the familiar playing of the waves the heavy flood of the night with the horror of its thousand despairings swelled up toward you, and you, who even now were the mistress, felt yourself lost. But then you gazed at the night, as before the sea; with glance and blood you made it into a partner; you tore out of the infinity of its directions the one, that which was yours, and you flung it as a bridge out of the core of your being into the core of the night. Then the horror disappeared; the great being turned its gaze upon you, and the sadness in it was to you, its kindred spirit, no more terrifying than the sadness in the eyes of your dog.

The infinite direction, the infinite tension, the infinite feelings mislead us, cause us to waver, deprive us of our rights. Then I set my inborn direction between them so that they distribute themselves around it as the mysteries of the night around the thrusting line of your glance, like the rock shapes here around the vertical of my body and my climbing step. The clouds of infinity, the waves that go between every pair of the numberless poles of the existent, confused my way; their number is infinite, and my way is one, like my direction. Nonetheless, their multiplicity is only the horizontal which intersects my vertical and I lifted their confusion from my life like the crossbeam from the cross. And that which bore me, now I bear it: as I bear my body.

The Woman: Were we not speaking just now of space? And now it is as if the words that you say are leading us into the spaceless.

Daniel: The words that *we* are saying. For is not your voice, when you are silent, the guest at my talking? . . . But already when we speak of space, we speak, in fact, of more than space. See, as the manifold sleep is set before the simple awakening, as the manifold horizontal before the simple vertical, so is the manifold Other set before the simple One, before the experience of connection.

The Woman: But is not the manifold the mother, the simple the son?

Daniel: Perhaps, but you do not come to the mother except through the son—when you go another way, you get lost. Since we cannot live without direction like eternal beings, there remains for us in the eternal only a single way: our direction. Not over the things, not around the things, not between the things—in each thing, in the experience of each thing, the gate of the One opens to you if you bring with you the magic that unlocks it: the perfection of your direction.

The Woman: You forget the power!

Daniel: No, for direction is only perfect when it is fulfilled with power: the power to live the whole event. Power alone would give you only the fullness, direction alone only the meaning of the life-experience; power and direction together allow you to penetrate into its substance, that is into the unity itself. Thus you find what is sought in vain in the track of the connections.

Look at this stone pine. You may compare its properties with those of other stone pines, other trees, other plants, establish what it has in common and what it does not have in common, explore what it is composed of and how it grew. That will be useful to you in the useful auxiliary world of names and classifications, of reports about how things arose and how they evolved. You experience nothing of the truth of this being. And now seek to draw near to this stone pine itself. Not with the power of the feeling glance alone—that can present you only with the fullness of an image: much, but not all. Rather, with all your directed power, receive the tree, surrender yourself to it. Until you feel its bark as your skin and the springing forth of a branch from the trunk like the striving in your muscles; until your feet cleave and grope like roots and your skull arches itself like a light-heavy crown; until you recognize your children in the soft blue cones; yes, truly until you are transformed. But also in the transformation your direction is with you, and through it you experience the tree so that you attain in it to the unity. For it draws you back into yourself; the transformation clears away like a fog; and around your direction a being forms itself, the tree, so that you experience its unity, the unity. Already it is transplanted out of the earth of space into the earth of the soul, already it tells its secret to your heart, already you perceive the mystery of the real. Was it not just a tree among trees? But now it has become the tree of eternal life.

The Woman: But what about when the connection is not the

ingeniously spun net of world-knowledge, but the deep element itself: the mother's lap in which we save ourselves from the cruel laws of isolation, the boundless into which we must dive from the shore of limits in order not to perish in contradiction? Is not all ecstasy a merging into the Other?

Daniel: It was said of Dionysus as Zagreus that the Titans enticed him by means of a game and tore him in pieces and devoured him. He who surrenders himself to ecstasy with undirected soul experiences this fate. The forces of chaos ravish him; the demonia of the unbecome explodes, dismembers his soul, and swallows it. In contrast, I might set the image of Orpheus who descended into the land of Hades with a lyre not in order to regain a beloved but in order to die and rise from the dead with Dionysus, who is Hades, completing the action of renewal in which that rhythm of breathing and of sleep is transfigured into sacrament. But this is the archetypal in Orpheus, that he enters into ecstatic death with the lyre. Not enticed: decided, and with the lyre.

Music is the pure word of the directed soul. Here is nothing more of the ingenious connection out of chained polarities into which the life-experiences are wedged and confined, but also the formless mixture and its lostness are banned from this kingdom. The directed soul alone rules here. It sets its inborn direction, sets the melody in the abyss, and the forces of the deep arrange themselves around it as the "wild beasts" around the playing Orpheus. . . . You come to the mother not otherwise than through the son.

The Woman: So direction is then the inner song?

Daniel: That the Orphic, the decided, the submerging and anew homecoming, the dying and becoming soul of magic has its song which it keeps intact, immortal in all death—that is the work of its direction. Yes, direction is itself altogether nothing else than magic.

A soul meets the shore of the world. Immediately the whirlpool of happenings plunges over it like an endless sandstorm that threatens to destroy it. It braces itself to withstand it. And see, therein is decided of what nature a soul is: how it withstands the whirlpool. The one thinks only of protection. It surrenders itself entirely to the inherited powers, the traditional arts of self-defense which educate its senses to perceive in place of the whirlpool an ordered world conceived within the framework of basic principles of experience. And indeed this *is* protection. For to the benumbed soul the divine force of the whirlpool is also benumbed. Not so the other. It finds no satisfaction in the protection that the inherited powers accord it. It lets it stand, to be sure, the auxiliary world in which alone it can live with men; it accepts it and learns its laws. But deep within it grows and endures the readiness to go out to meet the naked whirlpool. Armed with what? With nothing other than with the magic of its direction, its own, inborn, unique direction, belonging to it and no other. And now I may indeed encompass it in a verbal definition without having to fear that I shall injure your conception: Direction is that primal tension of a human soul which moves it to choose and realize this and no other out of the infinity of possibilities. Thus the soul strips off the net of directions, the net of space and of time, of causes and of ends, of subjects and of objects; it strips off the net of directions and takes nothing with it but the magic of its direction. That is the strength that the soul has found in itself, to which it recalls itself, which it raises out of itself. And see, dear, now the power of the directed soul proves itself. For the directionless god or demon, who does not need direction, may perhaps be blissful, and it is beautiful to think of him, breathing without direction, circling without direction, a directionless joy; but wretched is the undirected man who needs direction and must do without it, the powerless one. Powerful, however, is the directed soul, since it goes forth to meet the whirlpool, enters into the whirlpool. And such is its power that it charms it, magically charms it, so that it stands naked in the naked and is not destroyed. Rather it rests around the soul, as the sheath around the sword, as the earth around the grain of corn, as the mother around the child. And then the soul knows its mother's lap.

When man had succeeded in harnessing the happening in the machinery of cause and effect, when the machinery stood joined fast and the skillfully finished clockwork did its bidden service, then they named the swing of the pendulum irresistible necessity. To neither the joinings of human need between birth and the grave, however, nor to the fate of all life that is scattered abroad in the world, nor to all the counterplay of the elements, nor even to the movement of the stars themselves, not to all these investigated and registered things may I grant the name of necessity, but only to the directed soul. For as the needle of the magnet has chosen from all the points of the compass the north, and as my body has chosen from all positions the vertical, so the soul from the beginning has chosen its direction out of the fullness of the all-possible. But the magnet needle obeys, and each must point to the same; and even my body obeys and may only carry out in tension and consciousness what is bidden to all human bodies. The soul, in contrast, commands and has chosen not obeying but commanding, and it does not know where north is; rather its north is there where it points, and where it points there from eternity to eternity no other can point. And what the ages of the human race could do: to erect a structure of direction whereon nature regulates itself for the human senses, that the soul can surpass; for with its one direction it summons reality and conjures it, conjures it around its direction, so that the reality does not regulate but reveals and delivers itself, not to the senses and the understanding alone but from being to being and from mother to child. Thus the directed soul is the necessity of nature.

But direction is the necessity of the soul. And because my body is happy with my soul since its direction mirrors itself in your direction, I might here, standing between the rocks, sing a prize song to you, if I could do it properly. But, in fact, it can only be said in deeds, not in words, and it manifests itself only through its effect: it is that which pulls me up in the morning and drives me into the wilderness, which visits me at midday and sends me to the living, which takes my hand at evening and leads me to God—the high Lord of my all-solitude.

The Woman: . . . Give me your hand, Daniel.

Daniel: Here.

The Woman: ... What do you see?

Daniel. My hand in yours.

The Woman: A horizontal, is it not?

Daniel: A horizontal.

The Woman: Might you—might you remove the crossbeams?

Daniel: For nothing.

The Woman: How so?

Daniel: Because this is not the compulsion by the other which it is valid to overcome, but the choice of the other: the direction of the holy spirit, the flowering cross of community.

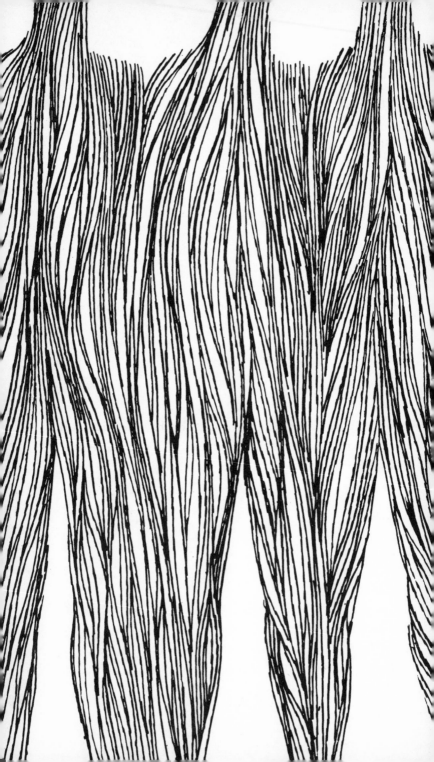

II On Reality. Dialogue Above the City

Ulrich: How the voices of the city die away! Only in this small stretch have we wandered from them, and already all their noise, which even now spurted up to us, has fallen into the great mixing bowl of distance, and of all the storms of its haste this rustle remains with us—almost a song.

Daniel: A song, Ulrich, a song! Yes, they tugged and shrieked like sick hounds on the chain, the goal-possessed thousand-times-thousand; they raged against and through one another, and still there throbbed unknown in each throat the longing for the song that is liberated now not in their ears but in ours. There was a moment when I heard it otherwise: in the midst of the tumult of the street, not a play of the distance, but the bleeding nearness, sung to me by the longing of the longing ones.

Ulrich: One moment?

Daniel: Do you not know what the moment which you allow to fulfill itself brings to you, what a flood of song and light? . . . I went among the crowd and thought of nothing other than opening my soul so wide to it, so to unbolt granary and treasure house that everything might find place in it of that open and hidden need of these men of which I could in any way be aware. I spoke within myself: What can I do for you, you who rush around me without purpose and touch me without understanding, nameless crowd? I have not the power to heal you and have not the art to comfort you; and if I sacrificed my life for you, nothing would be accomplished. But this I may do: receive you, gather your scattered pain in me, make your torn pieces whole in me, so that my soul may become your song, you songless one. And with this will I went through the crowd. And then this will became actual in me; it happened to me, so that I no longer knew myself but only a tumult of forces, hitting and rushing past one another without measure or way. But in the center of the tumult a heart dwelt, like a human heart, which received blood from the whirl and sent it again to all its corners. And the presence of this formless and unruly body at first so overpowered me that I performed my service like a pump, humble and stupefied. But then meaning came over me again, and I received from each of these forces, yes, from each of these galloping, purpose-mad forces—from the hungry and the greedy, from the seeking and the

62

grasping—rising from each, I received a song. O that pale, flickering, ghostlike singing! As I received it, I became faint-hearted, my friend, fainthearted with choking compassion, and no longer had any will in me other than this one—to be again a man and to take one of these men by the hand and say to him: "Remember, brother, that your soul is a free and mighty firmament that nothing can compel." Then I threw off and abjured my office, and already I stood again in my body, in the midst of the crowd. But I did so trembling and saw what was around me as a gigantic circling top, and my lips were struck dumb. Thus I stood trembling and mute, and after I had stood awhile, I went home and sat on a bench in the garden and was alone in a worse loneliness than ever before . . .

Only much later, however, was it revealed to me what I had known in that moment.

Ulrich: In that moment? How can you be so certain of that?

Daniel: You know certainly about what is called the sign in an act of knowing. You wake up one morning or you pause on a walk and you have a thought in your hands, a knowing thought that you see for the first time and yet which is as ripe and ready as if you had formed it over a very long time. But while you are regarding it, you notice that it bears a sign: it is an image out of a place and a moment and in it the seal of a life-experience. And whether you establish your knowledge in the holiness of a silence or offer it for sale on the market of words, the sign cleaves to it.

Ulrich: And perhaps it is this that allows us to feel our knowledge as something living and indestructible even when it is preserved in silence. . . . But what was it, Daniel, that you knew at that time?

Daniel: If I may say it to you as simply as I knew it: he remains unreal who does not realize.

Ulrich: You will probably have to say it to me more complexly if I am to understand it.

Daniel: Indeed, we already spoke once of the fact that there is a twofold relation of man to his experience: the orienting or classifying and the realizing or making real. What you experience, doing and suffering, creating and enjoying, you can register in the structure of experience for the sake of your aims or you can grasp it for its own sake in its own power and splendor. In so far as you fit it into the experience, you elaborate it according to the forms and laws of experience. It no more occupied a space than the new heaven which John saw at Patmos; but you make it into a thing in space, fix it in its place with the cipher of a column of air above it and the cipher of the earth's gravity below it, with an unshakably fixed relationship to each other point of the world. It was no more temporal than the last, already double-directed glance of the dying man; you make it into an event in time, expand it into a sequence, as a boy violently spreads out a rosebud, and then you shove it between a before and an after which squash it flat. It was no more causal than the majesty of the first dream; you force it into a chain where it represents just as much meaning as every other link in the chain: joining it as a link with another link. It was no more an object than God is an object to man or man to God: you break it in two so that you injure its core and with superior certainty name the pieces the perceiving and the perceived. But when it has been inserted in these and similar structures and machineries, so that the inserted parts fit with one another and it may be found in them again at any time, and when the sketch of insertions can be expressed in a generally understandable statement, then this statement is commonly called the truth. And to a certain extent rightly so; for doubt is at home on journeys of discovery, but truth and error are easily established in reading a map. Only one shall not speak of reality in all this.

Ulrich: Why, Daniel? Do you wish to assert that science, which is verified in natural happenings and in purposeful acts, is not built throughout on reality?

Daniel: I do indeed mean that. But understand me rightly. The structure of experience appears to me ingenious but not artificial; it seems to me an elaboration of life-experience, yet not an arbitrary one. It has still drawn all its forms and laws, yes its whole existence, determined by ancient goals, out of nothing other than precisely the eternal life-experience of man, and what it has established in regularities reflects deep rhythmic traits of life-experience, to be sure only symbolically. And how should I not honor this unsurveyable edifice of science and its wonderful development? How could I wish it away, wish to go back behind it, without transgressing against the power of the spirit? For everywhere where a knowing was formed, where it began, where it was creative, it was not orienting but realizing; immersion in pure life-experience, and what was thus found was carried over into the bed of enregistering. And everywhere where orienting knowledge ruled autonomously it was robbery, for it took place at the cost of the mothering, nourishing juices of life-experience and was only able to transpose the realization in the greater into a little need or a little security. And it is this predominance of the orienting from which I suffer and against which I rebel—for the sake of the realizing which creates out of the life-experience of reality.

Ulrich: Then you want to understand by reality not the elementary material of the life-experience but a work of the soul?

Daniel: A work of the soul certainly; but consider that in life-experience we are not offered a material that we form and that is detachable for our forming, extractable out of it; rather that it sprouts in our activity and that in the finished plant we can no longer in any way separate out the seed. Life-experience is only given to us to observe and compare in the form which our function, orienting or realizing, has developed out of it; in its unformed essence we only experience it, but we do not possess it. To our knowledge, to our memory, to our taking possession of it there lead from experience only the two bridges of our formation, and when it has crossed the bridge—even though its passage were faster than the speed of light—it is formed; it has become mere experience or reality. Life-experience is ungraspable like a lightning flash or a waterfall or the formation of crystals; we may not call it reality since we cannot thereby deal with it, draw it forth, and regard it. But still less will we accord the name of reality to the superstructure of experience.

Ulrich: But what do you think about the common usage of speech to which reality is simply the totality of the perceived and the perceivable which is experienced as the existing?

Daniel: It seems to me that we should pay attention to it because the life of men together is erected upon it, and not only for that reason. And we shall accept it again as soon as we have returned into the enclosure of the city, with a qualification, if that seems good to you, or unqualified. But now . . . has it not often struck you that in a poem, Hölderlin's perhaps, a word is employed in a heightened meaning that the common usage does not know?

Ulrich: In a poem certainly.

Daniel: And are not poems soaring knowledge? So let us now linger in a poem and call that reality which is to be called reality in a heightened meaning. And be sure that this heightened meaning, to which we now want to attend for a while, is even so little arbitrariness as the heightened meaning of the word in poetry. But this arises out of a no less deep necessity and a deeper legitimacy than the customary usage, which indeed corroborates the heightened meaning by subordinating itself to the poet after decades or centuries and adapting itself to his meaning. Why so? Because that heightened meaning stems from moments of heightened existence, heightened humanity, heightened knowledge. It is these that fix speech, renew speech. They must be taken into consideration when we wish to talk of reality and realization in a heightened, in a creative sense.

Ulrich: But how can we take them into consideration when they are inaccessible to us?

Daniel: Not more inaccessible than the hero is to the poet who knows him only because, having met with his face and his gesture in the world, he finds present in his soul what is expressed in this face and gesture . . .

Picture to yourself a man who remembers. I do not mean that resigned laziness which leaves the doors of the past open and turns to every entering shadow the same bittersweet attentiveness; also not that assumed superiority that reckons up what has been like the earlier moves of a game in which the decisive is still to be done; but also not that true and thankful accounting of a true man who judges the decisions and the absences of decision of his life. I mean the rarest of all, the heightened hour of great evocation when his lived life steps up to the testifying man like a form. See him, possessed by the shudder of the event, of the whole of which he has only now become fully aware; see him compose himself, govern his glance, behold. The image that he beholds is woven out of nothing else than out of that mysterious material that we call time, lived time. Out of the faces of lived time the holy countenance is unfolded, and the beholder recognizes this image which continually changes according to the meaning of life. What times, do you think, will he see again thus? Those in which he inserts his life-experience in the inherited structure of mediacy as a servant of the alien? Or those in which he catches them, as the ballplayer the ball, hurling himself against them, receiving them with hastily collected limbs; in which he embraces them, as the wrestler embraces the body tensed against him, throwing his whole strength into a muscle struggling for victory; in which he completes it as the runner his course, fulfilling, completing it with the swing of his own stride? Which, which does he recognize as reality, the hours in which the many overshadow and weaken the one or those in which the one shines in the undiminished fullness of its splendor because it is related to nothing other than to itself?

Yes, this is what it means to realize: to relate life-experience to nothing else but itself. And here is the place where the power of the human spirit awakens and collects itself and becomes creative. For where orientation rules, that crafty economy is at home whose shrewdness stinks to heaven because it only saves and never renews. But where the foot of realization stands, there power is drawn from the depths and collected and moved to action and renewed in work. As the ballplayer and the wrestler and the runner each is summoned by his task to draw all the force out of his body and pour it into the act, so life-experience calls to the man who is ready to realize it. For he may do that only as a whole and united person. And he who had only to register in the system of experiencing, and living with only one part of his being, could come to terms with the all, must now bring forth the totality of his being in order to withstand a single thing or event. But because the power gives itself in this way to the one thing, it becomes creative in it, creates reality in it, through it. For that alone is reality which is so lived. And all effective reality of the human world is lived thus, has been created thus.

Ulrich: Then it is so that what we call creating is only the expression of realizing? And the creative man is the realizing one?

Daniel: It is tempting, Ulrich, when one has recognized two forces of the soul as different, now also to construct two different classes of men and to lend to the first the one, to the second the other as their fixed and exclusive primal properties. But I can only imagine a creative man as one in whom that genuine iron ore that every, even the most miserable, human soul conceals becomes steel at red and then at white heat; only one in whom the spirit that is common to all fulfills itself unchecked in effective consequence. And in him as in all, the living encamps near the dead, only that in him the sunlike might of what is living makes what is dead fall into dust as we look at it. In him as in everybody, the growing borders on the stifled, the free on the warped, wisdom on folly—only that which lives with us counts for nothing else when the steel of genius flashes up into the air and strikes its blows. And so, a realizing kind of man, an orienting kind of man also do not exist. A purely realizing man would disappear in God; a purely orienting man degenerate into nothingness. Rather realization and orientation dwell close together, like conception and pregnancy, like knowledge and dissemination, like discovery and utilization. As in the life of the community the attained reality must ever again be inserted in the structure of experience, so in the life of the individual, hours of inserting follow hours of realization and must so follow; the solitary reality is still not only the highest of blisses but also the heaviest of burdens.

But in this you speak truly, that the name creative man belongs to him who has the most effective power of realization, to him in whom the realizing power of the soul has so concentrated into work that it creates reality for all. His realizing hours unite into a succession of summits of the eternal which shine forth out of the fleeting series of ups and down of his human life; even in his orienting the impulse of the actual lives on. For what belongs to man as a species before he lets himself be overrun by his aims, to primitive man, and what belongs to each individual man before he lets himself be overrun by his aims, that belongs to the creative man: the unbroken power of realization. But this power is strong in the primitive man and the child only because the orienting ability has not matured enough to be able to consume it; in creativity, in contrast, mature orientation is also included, but as a dependent and serving function. The primitive man and the child are *still,* the creative man *newly* master of reality. A moonbeam lies on the forehead of the former like a mirroring of a forgotten paradise, but the latter shines with the fire that it has stolen from heaven. They dream reality; it awakens it, the vigilant watchtower warder of the earth. And therefore the inner meaning of realization is revealed to him as to no other: that the realizing man is the genuinely real. For as the things that stand in his life-experiencing become reality, so also he himself.

Ulrich: But the things are still only real for the realizing man; for whom is he real?

Daniel: It would be very much preferable if we did not assert that the things are real "for him." Is the fire there for the iron or the iron for the fire or both only for the smith? No matter, the steel really comes forth and works. Realizing life-experience creates the essential form of existence of which we speak. What we call things and what we call I are both comprehended in what is thus created; both find their reality here; both can only find it here. For all life-experiencing is a dream of unification; orientation divides and sunders it, realization accomplishes and proclaims it. Thus all reality is fulfilled unification. Nothing individual is real in itself; everything individual is only preparation. The creative hours, acting and beholding, forming and thinking, are the unifying hours. The hero and the wise man, the poet and the prophet are unifying men. Communion is its mystery, and it is actual because it shares in the real, because in the times when it is highest, it is a real part. A something is not real for him, but with him; out of his life-experiencing, reality ascends that encompasses him. Reality for whom? For all, because out of it a seed of realizing falls in all? For a self that experiences us and receives from us nothing other than our reality? For no one? It does not matter: it *is,* and is not less if it is beheld by no eyes.

Ulrich: Then the creative man is thus a separate and select man?

Daniel: Only in the sense that in him there appears concentrated and effectively real what is sketched in all. In each man there dwells, utilized or suppressed, the power to become unified and to enter into reality. Yes, there are many, silent and unknown, who are equal to the creative in realizing power and yet do not reveal it in the world, whether because they lack the desire and art of far-reaching expression, because out of respect for the grace that has descended upon them they choose a life in a narrow circle and only become visible to what is near them, or because they are turned away and consecrated (for even the true hermit cannot persist without realizing power). These we may inscribe as the nameless on the tablet upon which the names of the creative stand—for the sake of their reality, because reality is splendid even when we only have a hint of it, but also for the sake of their effect, for the paths of effectiveness are a mystery, and it is often revealed to us in all stillness that the deeds of the secret ones are greater than the deeds of those who are in vogue.

Ulrich: Do you not think, too, Daniel, that those of whom you speak are few in our time?

Daniel: Realizing men are few in our time. It is busy replacing them by the producers.

Ulrich: The producers? Whom do you call by this name?

Daniel: Those who work without being, who give what they do not possess, who triumph where they have not fought: the pet children of appearance. They shun realization from of old or have renounced it when they take leave of their youth. But they do or make things such as once came only out of realization, or at least deceptively similar things. They do or make them brightly and with elegance; they do not demand, as realization did, that others join in their doing; they are satisfied that one recognizes them; how could one deprive oneself of them? God once created the world in six days, but since then we have learned the technique of creation. With its help the apes of God make the world in one day, and it is more interesting.

Ulrich: Why so bitter, Daniel? Let them be!

Daniel: Shall I not be bitter against the signature of this age? Do you not know the king who has installed these satraps? He is the same one who has stifled the power of realization in the bands of contemporary men. It is inborn in all of them in some strength, with some drive; and in all of them it does not attain to its height, and is hemmed in and destroyed and degraded. But the fact is that the power of realization cannot be injured by any earthly need or necessity; the only force which can attack and oppress it is the predominance of orientation. And that is the predominance that has insinuated itself into the blood of our age and dissolved its reality in order to put in its place its own brood, appearance. For before all other ages of civilization ours is the age that does not realize.

Look at this city that rushes along beneath us. Now dissolve also the contours of its image, and it lies under the veil of the evening distance as if it slept. But even in its sleep the fever of its days does not forsake it, and its dreams are like wanderings in the wilderness. Look, look through the veil: how beautiful it is, how strong, and how sick. For it has fallen to appearance.

The city, we say, but we do not, in fact, mean its houses and its factories, its wares and its refuse; we mean, in fact, these millions of men—not a number, Ulrich, forget the number, not a crowd, break up the crowd—all these individual men, naked underneath their clothes, bleeding under their skin, all these whose uncovered heartbeat united would drown out the united voice of their machines. These men are wronged, Ulrich, wronged in the right of rights, the gracious right of reality.

They have aims, and they know how to attain them. They have an environment, and they have information about their environment. They also have spirituality of many kinds, and they talk a great deal. And all of this outside of the real. They live, and they do not realize what they live. Their experience is ordered without being comprehended. They experience of it what component part it has in common with other experiences, and are oriented. To each of them eternity calls, "Be!" They smile at eternity and answer, "I have information." Their limitation is so closely cut to the body that they are glad and proud of it, and call it by elegant and pretentious names, such as culture, or religion, or progress, or tradition, or intellectuality: Ah, the unreal has a thousand masks.

Orientation is their lord—the spherical monistic or the conical theological or even only the waltz of the practical empiricism which helps in every need and removes all trouble. In the dead light of orientation, their destiny, which was summoned to experience living illumination in a living way and to become illuminated in itself, passes away. They walk as unreal men, hunt, storm after their aims. And, like the fiery columns of an evil demiurge, the aims stride before them and dupe them: but they plunge after, running and sliding past one another like an anarchic dance of specters.

Ulrich: But is our age really the only one so constituted? Were there not many before it?

Daniel: No age of history, Ulrich, could escape the leveling power of orientation, the registering, the utilizing. But always the great multitude of realizing men stood in their midst and dispensed warmth, movement, self-activity. The *terra incognita* was always beheld before it was measured, named, and enregistered. And even though man was long since overwhelmed by the ghosts of his aims and surrounded by the gigantic, in realization he had a dimension before whose threshold they remained standing and waited for the command of the wonderful wanderer. But an age came which succumbed to the superabundance of its material. That was the age when the aims themselves were surrounded by the means, numberless gnomes, each one of which now behaved like a tiny aim. And the soul stood opposite this swarming world of means, had to find its way in it, assert itself, protect its security. How could that take place? Through realization which, as one knew well, was full of insecurity and danger, profound and without safeguard? Could this infinitely developed life be mastered only on the strenuous, time- and strength-consuming detour of realization? Must this not be achieved more directly and without danger by orientation alone? They celebrated the great triumph of the investigation of nature in that they attributed to themselves the victory of realization, as the seneschal in the fairy tale replaced the sleeping dragon slayer. And thus the sin against the spirit took place, innocently and unforgivably.

Spirit is realization: unity of the soul, exclusiveness of life-experience, unification. But these men are yoked in the multiplicity of their aims, their means, their knowledge—everything is conditioned by everything, everything is decided out of everything, everything is related to everything, and over all there rules the security of orientation that has information. Yes, they have escaped the dangers of the deep. Concentrate oneself in life-experience? They concentrate in their work only their strength to work, and it succeeds; and their satisfaction means dispersion. Comprehend the life-experience in itself? If they could hunt up its contents on their map of heaven and earth, with names, neighborhood, length and breadth! Become united with a reality? They know that in this world one gets further by dissecting than by unifying, and what is needed by way of unification is taken care of at the same time by the competent retorts of orientation.

Ulrich: As much as I agree with you, there seems to me much that is immoderate in what you say, as though you meant all of the men of this city, and yet you know many and surely have an intimation of several who . . .

Daniel: Am I Yahweh and hold the punishing fire in my hands that I should enumerate the righteous? Or will it be pleasant to me to bear them in mind when this city is smitten with unreality? For the city, for the crowd, for the wretched millions my heart swells and revolts.

The unreal, the wretched! If my arm could only immerse them in the fire of renewal and baptize them to a second birth! If my mouth could only awaken the song the longing for which throbs unknown in each of these throats! If I could only redeem these specters to reality!

Ulrich: And do you think that the need and the contradiction, the wrong and the madness of the age when it is genuinely lived will become reality? That then all, as today the few, will know the great horror and the great compassion? That the flood of reality will tear down the dams of theories, of programs, of parties, and shake the innermost souls? That the realizing man must first of all realize the chaos?

Daniel: Yes, Ulrich! And only thus could he begin, begin again. For in the world of mankind there is no other beginning than reality.

Ulrich: Begin again, Daniel? Then we shall go back behind what this strange age, despite all its greatness, has given?

Daniel: No, rather all that must be genuinely conquered for reality in new, unheard-of battle. What now has its spectral existence in the deceptive game of unholy haste, in the distorted mirror of aims, in the illusory structure of information and false security, that shall—that must—Ulrich, become real, lived life. And that is life of immediacy and of human fellowship; for in genuine community as in genuine solitude it is immediacy which alone makes it possible to live the realizing as real.

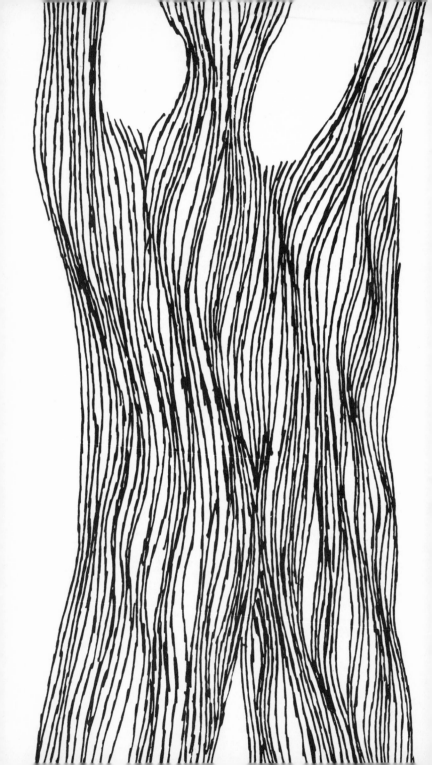

III On Meaning. Dialogue in the Garden

Daniel: Quick and young as the unexpected stride, I heard your
stride along my garden wall, and you did, indeed, come unexpectedly,
Reinold. Never before have you visited me in the morning.
You are welcome; I could only say that to a few at this hour.
For how many friends might stand in the face of the awakening
garden? The trees condemn him who is not upright and attentive;
the flowers judge him who does not open himself and submit
himself to the sun; and he who does not know the peace of
becoming, against him every blade of grass raises itself like a
flaming sword.

Reinold: You praise me for the first time, Daniel. I have often thought of how it would be if you praised me once, and how I should be glad of it. And now you praise me, and so much, and I cannot be glad. For I know that I do not stand before your garden. The peace of becoming, you say—I no longer know any calm. Rather restlessness and wandering and the worst anxiety —these have become my comrades.

Daniel: How has this happened to you, Reinold? For that this is something foreign to you, you also feel even now.

Reinold: O that I could only confess it to you. I have come in order to speak with you about it, but now that I am here I am ashamed. When I was a child, I once came running to my mother and called to her that I had caught a fish. She looked up at me, and I saw only then that she sat at the weaving loom. Then my beautiful fish became entirely insignificant to me before the mystery of the appearing and disappearing threads—and as often as I recalled that since then, I had to be ashamed.

Daniel: Just speak, you do right in doing so. So long as one is in the calm of his becoming, the Thou that he bears in himself may be enough for him. But when the flood comes to him, then his need and summons is to find the Thou to whom he can speak in the world.

Reinold: You read to us once a Celtic song; in it were a pair of verses that struck me as though I had long known and forgotten them:

> You do not tarry long wandering
> In the land with the living heart.

That was my childhood, Daniel: the land with the living heart. As the warm body has its heart that collects and distributes all the blood, and here the movement of the saps is set by center and unity, so the life of the child had a heart: it had an inexpressible, inexpressibly real meaning which was center and unity for it. A meaning, Daniel, one single, own meaning. And you must know that I was not at all lost in reverie, as other children probably are; and still the meaning was with me. It came just from nowhere, it was there, and I felt it as one feels his heart: there you are, deep-rooted in me, familiar, adventurous, small secret sun of this wonderful world! Meaning, meaning—the falling stars of the August nights had it not more and not less than the cut-off hair that I saw fall down on me; the narrow, immeasurable horizon of my space and my time was golden-rimmed with meaning. Nothing meaningless happened to me. When I awakened out of the music of my dreams into the dark, the night had my mother's arms and even motherly words like hers, and when a heavy illness befell me, the otherwise invisible ones were with me as guests and the plane on which I had lived rounded itself for me to a sphere.

And the things, the things, Daniel: the concaveness of the things was in my senses; the things clung close within it as the peach in the hollow of the hand. All beings and all events were in accord, more and otherwise than an account balances, more and otherwise than a song harmonizes; everything was attuned with me, everything concurred, everything was in accord out of its united self. Life did not at all appear to me peaceable and accommodating because of that; but hardness and sharpness, conflict and misfortune were like the fixed moves in a game that includes all kinds of moves in its rules and precisely thereby is meaningful.

So I was secure, Daniel, at ten years, at twelve years, at sixteen years, securer in the world than when I drank my mother's milk; at ten years, at twelve years, at sixteen years, secure with the security of the ruling one. And I stepped out of my childhood without stepping out of my security. I learned to know the overly bright duality of life, enmity and love, and the *meaning* did not fade for me. Out of my world, not out of a strange one came the enemy toward me, came woman toward me, and he was not the opponent, she was not the temptress, but both joined with me in arteries and veins which flowed into that heart, the meaning. And I was not soft to the one, not comfortable with the other, but in the midst of anger and longing both were primally and eternally familiar. Thus my eighteenth, my twentieth, my twenty-third year streamed and rested in the security of being in harmony and ruling. I was no longer a child, but around me there played at every hour a happy child, my sister, the world; and as long as she was near me and I was turned to her, nothing could harm me.

Someone other than you might ask me what has "happened" since then. But you once said to us that the decisions dwell not in the rise but in the dip of the folds, and so you will understand me.

This spring on my journey home out of the south I came one evening to Spezia. I had wanted to travel on throughout the night, but the sight of the sea was so powerful that it foolishly struck

me to want it despite my intention. I descended, went to the
harbor, took a small boat and rowed out. It was a new moon,
but from the depths above me a chorus of southern stars sang
down on me; my oar cut dark flood and concealed splendor;
boundlessness was the bed of my soul, heaven, night, and sea
its cushion. It was one of the hours in which we no longer know
more strongly what we do than what is done about us and
with us. So as I now turned the boat and returned to the shore,
I was barely conscious of the action of my hands.

Now I looked up casually—and was terrified. Everything that I
had just now possessed had disappeared. Out of a dumb infinity an
army of jack-o'-lanterns stared into empty infinity; threateningly,
thousands of moist lips, sneering cruelly, opened and closed
about me, and in the nape of my neck, dark and tangible as a
betrayal, the presence of the night beings grew. Where the bed of
my soul had been, was the nothing; seduced, betrayed, rejected,
my soul hung in the grey of the night between sea and heaven.
I did not understand, but I steeled myself for battle: "I am
there, I am there," I cried, "and you cannot annihilate me," and
strength spurted into my shoulders and my legs at the same time,
and gripped, with the feet firmly planted and the oars out: to the
shore!

Then a shrill conflict of light swept over a piece of the shore
and tore it loose. Shamelessly it stood stretched out from out of
the darkness and bellowed the nonsense of its clarity out over
the flood. Clarity—but I did not recognize it; bold and strange
it sprang out of the night as out of a black house door. And

85

already the night swallowed it again; and for a moment I could compose myself and *knew* all: the approaching storm and the cruiser over yonder that was using its searchlights. But when immediately thereafter the cold lightning bit into the land, my knowledge was of no use to me. Spectral stretches of earth detached themselves from one another before me in a senseless service; not like parts of a shore, but like spectral shrieks. I "knew" that they were connected, a busy and friendly little land, and knew the hearty smacks of the fishermen's children in their cradles and the stamping of the sailor's hornpipe in the tavern; but I *felt* no connection, rather shriek, shriek, and in between them the abyss.

The abyss was between piece and piece of the world, between thing and thing, between image and being, between the world and me—when the light of the searchlight came. And the feet firmly planted, with working arms, rowing to the known shore, surrounded by the shrill of the spectral truth, I longed for comfort like the dying Christ for the communion, and my benumbed soul longed for its sacrament, for *meaning:* for the meaning had burst, a bloody tear ran right through the middle of it. And I saw the ultimate: in me, in my inmost self, was the abyss. I was forever divided; not into spirit and body, as joined and detached in each other as ever, but in the thousandfold, Protean doubleness of the bright One and the dark Other, with the eternal abyss in between. There my last security shattered; broken I set foot on the shore, and when I set foot on the shore, it was to me a discordant, disjointed life. Behind me the storm rose over the sea, before me lay the calm land; but it was to me as though I now left the last, fearful hiding place of calm and entered into the harsh storm that would never end.

Since then the abyss is before me at all times—the nameless that everything that is named proclaims.

And it is strange, Daniel: when I had security, men appeared to me at times insecure in their questions and doubts; but now that I have lost my ground, they stand around me in superior equilibrium, like the sober around the drunk. And yet they know about the abyss; but they also have information. And they are not stingy with their information.

There are the world-knowers. That is the abyss between the things and the consciousness, they say; and this abyss is an illusion, for consciousness is a power among powers, and all is one. But what good does it do me that they deny what I have experienced with my being? Shall the truth verify itself to me in a finished agreement, instead of in the totality of my life-experience?

And there are the God-knowers. That is the abyss between man and God, they say; and at a certain place on a certain day it has been filled up for each one who henceforth believes in this filling up. Thus it is not filled up for me; for me it must be filled up here and now since I behold it here and now. Here and now is infinity and eternity like only nowhere and never; and here and now is the abyss. And I should rather behold it on all days and in all dreams and even in the hour of my death than smear my eyes with its salve and become blind to my truth.

And there are the mind-knowers. That is the abyss between the idea and the experience, they say; that is the abyss above which it is our office to build a bridge. And they build bridges out of transparent luster, the most beautiful in the world. But thought alone can set foot on these bridges; under every other step they break down. And it is not, indeed, my thought that beholds the abyss, it is my *being:* this thing made of stone and storm and flood and flame, this whole, weighing down, springing upward— this substance. There it stands, the elemental, and smiles at the beautiful bridges on which its child, thought, may dance.

And there are the knowers of mysteries. That is the abyss between the world of appearance and the true world, they say; we fly over it with our mystery. And truly, they have an airship, a wonderful one built out of sheer mystery; it ascends resoundingly, straight up into the air. It took me with it, and I felt wonderful, as though behind all the heavy seriousness there must still hide only a plaything. And so it was. For when we were again below, they said: Now we are on the other side. That seemed strange to me, for it was all like this side. And when I looked closely, I noticed that we stood on the same spot as before. Then I went my way.

And now I have come to you, Daniel, to learn whether you can tell me what I should do.

Daniel: Imagine a wanderer who on a deep, cloudy night after long wandering comes into the outermost street of an unknown city. Hour after hour he has walked in the empty darkness of the heath, no presence about him except that of the meager thickets; now he steps into the midst of another darkness, one that is filled to the rim with strange, threatening life. The houses stand like vague monsters with staring eyes and insidiously open jaws; between the houses the unknown extends, and the lights that flicker in the misty foreground are unsteady like the signals of a gang of murderers. No step is in the street, no sound; but its silence seems treacherous and its forsakenness like something lying in wait. Behind the hazy visible, from every quarter in the overfull invisible, danger gathers, slides, waltzes. And in the anxious heart of the wanderer one longing is powerful—for security. And because he longs for security, he needs above all else this one thing: to know his way about. What sort of a city is this? Where does this street lead? How do I get out of this sinister place? To know one's way about—that is the key to salvation and health, to security itself.

Of such nature is the longing of those who, seized by the shudder of the boundless or by the glimpse of the contradiction, only wish to protect themselves. Their being has become mature for knowledge, the mystery has opened itself to them, but they do not prepare themselves to withstand it. The irrational makes them anxious; instead of *realizing* it, receiving it into life-experience with the whole strength of the moment, they strive only to guard their security. All living with the whole being and with unconstrained force means danger; for there is no thing, no relation, no happening in the world that thus known does not reveal its bottomless abyss, and all thinking threatens to shatter the stability of the knower. But danger is what they wish to avoid; they will not risk their skin for the sake of a vain problematic. They want security, and security once for all. He who lives his life in genuine, realizing knowledge must perpetually begin anew, perpetually risk all anew; and thus his truth is not a having but a becoming. But they want to know where they are; they do not want to be under way but at home; they want to be provided for and insured; want a solid general truth that will not let itself be overturned; want only to know their way about, want only to *orient* themselves in the world, that is, protect themselves in the world. So they build their ark or have it built, and they name the ark *Weltanschauung,** and seal up with pitch not only its cracks but also its windows. But outside are the waters of the living world.

But set another wanderer in that place and let the same street, the same hour envelop him. He goes, he remains standing, he turns himself, with wide-open senses, with opened spirit, willing and firm. He does not want to know his way about; how could he ever experience of this here more than now and thus? He wants only to live this here—the wild darkness, the fallow, animal faces of the houses and the reeling lights in the depths—so completely that it becomes for him reality and message. Of what value is it to him what city this is? Here it speaks to him in another tongue than in that in which names exist. What does it mean to him where this street leads? Now he is in it, truly in it, and may not be elsewhere. It is not sinister to him; does not the indefinite proclaim existing being just as faithfully as the definite? Does not the insidious attest to the holy power as fervently as the reliable?

***World view. [Translator]**

He is no less turned to the compressed breath of the lurking than the even breath of the sleeping. He knows danger and will meet it when it is demanded; he has a strong wrist and knows how to defend himself; but what would life be if it did not everywhere approach the uttermost and threaten to capsize? The script of life is so unspeakably beautiful to read because death looks over our shoulder.

Such is the way of him who forgets himself in order to practice realization according to his strength. He does not long for the security of knowing his way about, which can only succeed when the life-experience is not lived to its ground, when only the surface is taken from it, that which can be rationalized and ordered; he loves danger and the underived truth which he who ventures draws from the depths. He does not want to know where he is; how could he, for he is not always at the same place but is ever at the new, ever at the uttermost. Ever at God, I may even say, since God cannot, in fact, realize himself in man otherwise than as the innermost presence of a life-experience, and for him therefore it is not the same, but ever the new, the uttermost, the god of this life-experience. Orientation, which acts as the all-embracing, is thoroughly godless; godless also is the theologian who fixes his God in causality, a helping formula of orientation, and the spiritualist who knows his way about in the "true world" and sketches its topography; all religiousness degenerates into religion and church when it begins to orient itself: when instead of the one thing needful it provides a survey of what one must believe in this life and the beyond, and promises having instead of becoming, security instead of danger.

All security which is promised, all security which is longed for and acquired, means to protect oneself. It is that which is promised and allotted to the believers of all old and new churches. But he who loves danger and practices realization does not want to protect himself but to realize himself. He is the unprotected in the world, but he is not abandoned; for there is nothing that can lead him astray. He is not at home in the world, yet he is at home at all times; for the ground of each thing wishes to harbor him. He does not possess the world, yet stands in its love; for he realizes all being in its reality. He knows no security yet is never unsure; for he possesses steadfastly that before which all security appears vain and empty: direction and meaning.

The wanderer who remained standing was not oriented and did not want to be; he did not know the name of the city into which he had entered, what the place was called, where the street led; but when he walked further, his step did not hesitate, and when he came to a crossroad, he chose with immediate decision as out of a deep command. He who has direction does not have information as to how the will is determined in cause and effect, nor as to what one must hold to be good and bad, nor that there is an evolution in which one is imprisoned; but when he acts, he does his deed and no other, he chooses his lot and no other, he decides with his being. The secure man is entangled in the net of his system of orientation; his action stands on its spot in world and time and has no more space than this spot affords it; it is limited before and after by evolution, for how could he trust himself to do that which evolution has not authorized him to do? But he who has direction and practices realization, to him the deed is not limited by causality and evolution; he feels himself free and acts as a free man. Let the orienting man call his freedom the illusion of subjectivity, let him prove the conditioned nature of his deed and describe its origin: everything may be presented afterward that is not a part of his reality; all revolution sees that which comes afterward as evolution. But to him who ever begins anew the deed is as magic is to the primitive man: as the magic action does not hang in a chain of happenings but is a world event which begins and ends out of itself, as there on the path from working to effecting the whole expresses itself and the ring closes itself, so he who ever begins anew does the deed out of itself into being as an act of creation and a completion. This is direction: the magic power of unconstrained acting which wants to realize itself and chooses its deed with the being.

And over it the star shines down *meaning* and sends its beam into all happening.

The wanderer who remained standing in the outermost street and did not hesitate at the crossroads, came to a place around which grew plane trees; he sat down beneath one of them and looked up at the heavens. At this moment the clouds parted, and a solitary, very bright star appeared to the eyes of the man, who greeted it like a brother. "All the time you were turned to me," he said, "and now I *see* you too, distant and friendly one, ever present one!" And in the light of the star all his wanderings timelessly arose for him in great truth, together with the heath and the road and this place between the plane trees, living deeply in its own meaning, as a myth of being and a revelation.

Meaning is not, like the ark of those who protect themselves, constructed out of planks, with joints sealed up with pitch, but is singly created out of the material of the element, like the fiery chariot which carried Elijah away. One cannot scrape it together out of experiences of just any kind, nor does it let itself be taught and transmitted; rather it is joined to the soul as a primal possession, to be unfolded and verified in its life-experience. And as the painter who singly wills the painting still accomplishes the work as an expression of the spirit and as witness of his daimon, so the soul itself that wills nothing else than genuinely to live from the ground and to establish reality transfigures the lived world in the light of meaning into a holy mirror in which the sign of primal being appears. Orientation installs all happening in formulas, rules, connections which are useful in its province but remain cut off from a freer existence and unfruitful; realization relates each event to nothing other than its own content and just thereby shapes it into a sign of the eternal. As in his deed so too in his knowledge, the man who stands in the love of the world is related to the primitive man, to the myth-creating man: as in myth a significant event of nature or mankind, say the life of a hero, is not registered in a knowable connection but is preserved as something precious and consecrated in itself, adorned with the pride of all the spheres and elevated as a meaningful constellation in the heaven of inward existence; and as there in its exalted solitude it becomes a symbol of all fate and a mirror of the faintly sensed world-spirit, so he who stands in the love of the world does not know a part of a continuity but an event which is fully complete and formed in itself, as a symbol and seal which bears all meaning. This is meaning: the mythical truth of the unconstrained knower who relates to each event in its content alone and thus shapes it to a sign of the eternal. He receives that which befalls him as a message; he does what is necessary for him as a commission and a demonstration.

And thus according to man's concepts he has no image of the world; in fact, he has one that is as immediate as Veronica's handkerchief: in his life. He does not know the world and does not know whether one can know it; but the unknowable is authenticated for him as one lived in him and through him. For like the primitive man, who has in magic his essential deed, in myth his essential knowledge, and celebrates them as both covenant with and festival of the mystery in which he conquers separateness and unites himself with the God, so he who has direction and meaning celebrates an ever-new mystery in his realizing: to live so as to realize God in all things. For God wills to be realized, and reality is God's reality, and there is no reality except through the man who realizes himself and all being.

This is the kingdom of God, Reinold: the kingdom of danger and of risk, of eternal beginning and of eternal becoming, of opened spirit and of deep realization, the kingdom of holy insecurity.

Security—thus you name the breath of your first life. But that was not the security of those who protect themselves and know their way about. That was the security of the sleepwalker. Children are sleepwalkers in the world. They pass through all abysses unharmed, for they do not see them. The direction that guides their steps is dreamlike, the meaning in which everything fulfills itself for them is dreamlike. Dreamlike they realize their life-experience. It is granted them to realize without risk because they are unaware of the inner duality and therefore all things also offer themselves to them undivided. Everything harmonizes with them like a roundelay, and the contradiction itself joins in the play. If God wants to appear to them, he must disguise himself as a traveling musician and put on a foolish face.

Then comes the hour of awakening. It can come late. There are men whose realizing power is so great that it outlasts childhood in its first form—the dreamlike simplicity. No matter: it happens that an abyss that one has countless times passed by suddenly looms at his feet. The abyss of contradiction and of opposition: the abyss of the thousand-named immanent duality of all things. It calls to him out of the deep, and then he knows that an abyss in himself answers, it too thousand-named: the abyss of his inner division. Thus he is afraid. And in his fear the choice is placed before him: to which will he give the power, orientation or realization. This is not a question of delivering himself wholly to one: neither can exist without the other; it is a question of mastery. Orientation promises him security. Realization has nothing to promise. It says: If you wish to become mine, you must descend into this abyss. What wonder is it if the choosing man hands himself over to the friendlier mistress and only now and then, in the rare hours of self-recollection, casts a melancholy glance at the other?

You have decided, Reinold, whom you do not want to follow. Thus you have also already decided whom you want to follow. You have known from of old what you must do, and you also know it now; for direction is with you as of old. But this is the time when your first, dreamlike strength is at an end and your second, awakened strength wants to commence. There you stand irresolute and lost in thought as though you listened to a distant call. Still the fact that you have today spoken with me is your first new step. Now you again know your way.

Meaning appeared to you to be burst, Reinold. That is because it wanted to renew itself. In the dreaming heart a daring heart was enclosed that wants now to arise, wants to awaken from its larva life to a winged life. The duality of the world was enveloped for you in the light of meaning; it advanced toward you out of it; now you shall envelop it anew in resurrected light. Thus meaning is reborn for you, and nothing can injure it henceforth.

Dreamlike until now the peace of your becoming, and now it is disturbed by restlessness and wandering. You must win it anew, and as an awakened one. It had light feet and a flowerlike glance, and it knew nothing of danger. Now you are dragged out with it and visited by dangers. And from every path it will return with stronger longing and steadier eyes. But be comforted: its feet will not unlearn the dance and its glance the caress.

Danger, danger, danger: that is from now on your path. "God and the dreams," so goes a song, Reinold, the song of the happy early ones. But your motto will be: God and danger. For danger is the door of deep reality, and reality is the highest price of life and God's eternal birth.

And if the poets of the age should surround me and each ask me: "Have I not imagined the most beautiful life?" then I would answer: The most beautiful life that has been imagined is the life of the knight Don Quixote who created danger where he did not find it. But more beautiful still is the lived life of him who finds danger in all the places where it is to be found, and it is to be found in all places. All creation stands on the edge of being; all creation is risk. He who does not risk his soul can only ape the creator.

Live upright and attentive, opened and devoted in the peace of your becoming, Reinold, and love danger. You have no security in the world, but you have direction and meaning, and God, who wants to be realized, the risking God, is near you at all times.

And this is your *nearest* danger: descend into the abyss! Realize it! Know its nature, the thousand-named, nameless polarity of all being, between piece and piece of the world, between thing and thing, between image and being, between the world and you, in the very heart of yourself, at all places, with its swinging tensions and its streaming reciprocity. Know the sign of the primal being in it. And know that here is your task: to create unity out of your and all duality, to establish unity in the world; not unity of the mixture, such as the secure ones invent, but fulfilled unity out of tension and stream, such as will serve the polar earth—

the realized countenance of God illuminated out of tension and stream. But know too that this is the endless task, and that here no "once-for-all" is of value. You must descend ever anew into the transforming abyss, risk your soul ever anew, ever anew vowed to the holy insecurity.

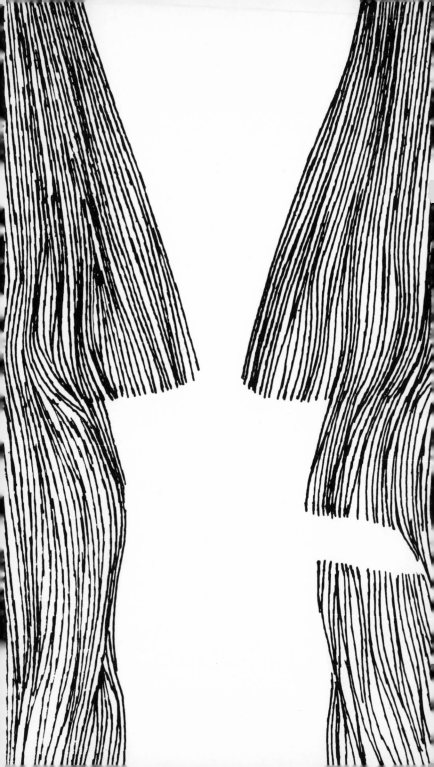

IV On Polarity. Dialogue After the Theater

Leonhard: Did the play move you so, Daniel? As you walk next to me, imprisoned in silence, it feels to me as if we did not come the same way: I certainly from the theater, but you from Eleusis.

Daniel: I come from the theater, Leonhard, and what has moved me and set me into a silence is the theater itself. I saw it today for the first time.

Leonhard: You jest.

Daniel: Has it not happened to you that you were acquainted with a man for many years and had him in and next to you, familiar as a word that you always have at hand and believe you know— although it has never occurred to you to regard it—and on an evening when the lamp between you and him stands in a new corner, you see him for the first time, and you are seized by wonder; for in the lines and proportions of the familiar face you recognize an unfathomable, significant secret—a ground line and ground proportion of life.

Leonhard: And today you have seen the theater thus?

Daniel: When I came in, it had just become dark. How often already had I entered the auditorium at this moment, and it had only added to my enjoyment that I did not need to see anyone before the performance began, and came out of the lax light of the street directly into this severe light, out of the wild dice game of the street directly into this regulated checker game. This time it was different. In the darkness the event took hold of me. Eleusis, you say; indeed, it might have been thus with the consecrated when the lights were extinguished. And then the curtain went up.

Leonhard: But it was just then that the play began, the play that I, sitting not far from you, have seen and heard.

Daniel: The play? Yes, somehow also the play; or, if you will, first there began, in fact, only the play. But it made itself felt so that something took place before me in a way that seemed to me unusual and astonishing. In a space that was lifted out of the context of space and no longer had any connection, neither with the above nor with the below, neither with the right nor with the left, neither with the behind nor with . . . but yes, a single, specific connection with this before where I was. In a time that was detached from the course of time and fulfilled itself without before and after, and in each moment was so filled with impetus and significance that it seemed to me that before and after had been emptied in order to fill this bulging vessel, the moment.

Leonhard: But all round was still, indicated by the contrivances of the real space, the imaginary space out of which the men of the drama came and into which they returned, and into the drama there drifted and stormed, whispered and beckoned the imaginary before, the earlier life of these men!

Daniel: It was not so to me. Rather, when they appeared to me, they came from the edge of being, and when they went, they died away into the void, as a tone dies away. They announced to me nothing other than their presence. And they did this with the precision of a shadow.

Leonhard: How am I to understand you?

Daniel: Look at the ground, at the shadows of the trees as they stretch themselves over our path. Have you ever seen in the upper world of the trees a branch so outlined, so clear, so abstract as here? Is that not the branchness of the branch? Shadows—and first of all I saw what I saw today in the theater like a shadow play: like an overly clear and still somehow unclear play. The intellectual prologue passed me by; I knew and did not know what happened.

I was like the youth in that fictitious issue of the Sopater. Do you recall it? He has dreamed that he is consecrated to Eleusis and that he sees the holy rites. Awake he tells a friend, a consecrated one, what he has seen and asks him whether it corresponds to the actual mystery. The friend nods. Has he now betrayed the holy rites to an unconsecrated man? No; for the dreamer had been consecrated by the goddesses themselves, Demeter and Kore, and as a consecrated one he had experienced all. And yet he did not know; for he had not understood the voice of the hierophant, and so the ultimate meaning of the symbol remained unclear to him.

But suddenly I understood the voice that spoke within me. And this all at once, as though the stage of this day before which I sat had been transformed into the Christian mystery stage where the throne of heaven stood over the human room, under which gaped the great devil's maw of hell and the axis goes from pole to pole through the heart of the poor sinners.

Yes, what I saw was the spectacle of duality. But not good and evil; all valuation was only external dress. Rather the primal duality itself, being and counterbeing, opposed to each other and bound to each other as pole with pole, polar opposed and polar bound—the free polarity of the human spirit. There outside in the world of the lax light that I had left when I entered into this kingdom of the severe, there outside the two were enveloped by mediacy and unrecognizable; but here they stood naked and large as gods, naked their gestures, naked their voices. A mediating chorus of figures surrounded them, but they stepped forth from the mediating circle only clearer, more inaccessible still. What they did only unfolded what they were; the streams that ran back and forth between them only expressed but did not weaken the polar strength of their being thus; and what truly stood in the center between them was not something mediating but the I of the spirit whose primal secret duality they revealed.

Leonhard: The play affected you so strongly?

Daniel: The play . . . yes, it was certainly the play.

Leonhard: It was performed with unusual force.

Daniel: Yes, the performance too. . . . But at that time I knew nothing of play and performance. What happened to me at that time in the detached imaging to which my senses fastened was of so elemental a nature that I sensed no intention, no production, no arrangement; rather the happening that bestowed itself on me thus was immediately certain. But the two, the polar protagonists, had made a daimon—indeed, who then might know the silent names of the daimons! Now then, the daimon of the theater had magnified them for me. The cothurnus of the myth was strapped to their feet; out of their dialogue resounded the antiphony of *ananke.** There they stood, the tragic pair, like Creon and Antigone, and had neither right nor wrong, neither guilt nor innocence, had nothing except their being, their polarity, their destiny. And I felt world-great before them, as though I were the I of the spirit whose primal secret duality they revealed. But already I was no

* **Greek concept of irrational, irreducible necessity. [Translator]**

105

longer before them, rather truly in their midst, and the streams that ran from pole to pole ran through my heart.

Then the curtain fell, the lights blazed up, a festive, well-meaning light, fit to mediate between that of the street and that which had now disappeared. I sat in the midst of the audience and found it difficult to know where I was.

Leonhard: I know . . . I nodded to you, and you greeted me in return, but as if you did not know me.

Daniel: Certainly I did not know you. I knew nothing except just that audience, but that truly and wonderfully.

I had, in fact, experienced what was the first act of my drama not as one of the spectators but as a secret hierophant; now the crowd of which I was a part surprised me and filled me with astonishment as though I had associated with it for the first time. These men had separated themselves out and combined; they had installed themselves in the solitary space, in the solitary time of this stage and accepted its procedure as something allied to them; with different meanings, to be sure, the one stirred to action, the other aware of the performance, only a few conjoined in that dynamic wholeness* in which the action and performance are submerged in a mythical reality, as symbol and preparation, but open to all that is happening to the actor, answering the symmetry of his step with the symmetry of the soul's step and, whether with resigned, whether with superior feeling, mastering a task.

* Literally "in that dynamic wholeness of being-with (Mitsein)." [Translator]

So that "manifold and innumerable throng" was really like
Eleusis which had represented the marriage of heaven and earth
and the birth of God's son; and if they did not "regard as a
salvation" what was presented, if their attitude was almost as
profane as the chatting of their intermissions, they were still,
as long as the stage spoke, united and revealed participants.

Their profanity did not withstand me. I still carried in myself the
measure of that completed polarity in which I had stood for a
while, like the measure of a passion that supplements everything
fragmentary and broken around it to wholeness, rather lets it
appear in its wholeness. So my surroundings grew together for me
into a community of which I was a member. And thus, no longer
as focus and center but as a member, I experienced the second act
of my drama.

I perceived, as the member of a settlement of madrepores may
perceive, with the organs of the community; but at the same
time this whole had become for me so unitedly present as a single
being is present to himself in his consciousness. So, therefore,
I found it, I found *myself* over against that other being who moved
on the stage and conversed with himself. For without its weakening
its inner cleavage, indeed at the very time when it had become
more lively and stood more in relief, that polar world of the
agon had also won the shape of a being. It stood over against
my We-I, as the storm the stillness, the mountain of waves
the sandy plain, the contradiction the agreement. But in all its
multiplicity it still appeared to us now as a being like us, determined
by a law and held together in its contradiction as we in our

agreement. And so we extended ourselves over against each other, divided by the severe light of the footlights—space and frame, time and scene, agreement and decision, audience and tragedy— being and counterbeing.

Yes, being and counterbeing! For both stood in a polar relationship like those two on the stage; only they were less distinct because, crossing and troubling them, one other oscillated with them that I knew without being aware of it: the polarity of "appearance" and of "reality."

Being and counterbeing: but they were not set in opposition to each other as the two in the drama who now appeared to be enclosed in a unity; they did not carry out their polarity as those did. Each persevered in its calling, the one in happening, the other in perceiving. And this perceiving seemed to me no less notable than that happening. For it did not behave with that well-meaning neutrality that the observer commonly brings to the observed. Rather it bore its oppositeness in itself, in some way expressed, confirmed it; and not just one part of that which had been divided in two but the whole reality over against it. Therefore it sided with no party; it was, as it were, itself a party which met those two as a unity. But what a strange party which was nothing but perception! Or perhaps still more than this? Yes, something else was there: confirmation. And confirmation, indeed, not of the mediating chorus that also lived through the happenings on the stage, but of the contradiction, the destiny, the decision. There stood the two in the fury of their nature; there the fate worked itself out between them; and here sat the audience and confirmed, strengthened, affirmed; perceiving the fate, it willed what it experienced. This awareness was a proclamation.

Where had I already seen something like this? I recalled; it was a crude early Greek vase-picture that shows the psychostasia. Two heroes in battle, and behind them Hermes weighing the souls. Coarsely as it is painted, one sees: he does not take sides but his will follows the decisions of the scales; he wills what must happen, and his will is a fanfare.

How this image appeared before my eyes, however, the difference between that and Hermes, agitated me violently. Yes, when on the stage the murdering knife is raised, the heart of this dark being, the audience, palpitates in the knife's point; but it quivers at the same time in the flesh that receives the blow. It joins with the fate that guides the hand of Oedipus, and it lives in the blinded eyes. It swings along with that wave that drives Lear to his madness; it circles in the pain of the king, mad like him.

And now I also saw it more clearly than before: before the great play all of them, those stirred to action and those aware of the performance, had a single heart in common. From the one fell off the firmness of his resignation, from the other the seeming force of his superiority; they became one in the act of inclusion.

For thus one may perhaps name what happened here. A being stands over against his counterbeing; it expresses, accompanying the impact of his fate, his polar being; but at the same time it throws itself across into his opposite pole and suffers his life with him. How shall one name this remaining with oneself and setting out, this desire to attack, and joy in sacrifice, this bipolar living? I say inclusion and know that I say too little. But allow me the word; for when I utter it I have another polarity in mind, and the loving man is present to me who has a living experience not only of his struggling desire but also of the blossoming beloved and includes what is opposite him as primally his own.

The falling curtain called me out of these thoughts. Again the festive, well-meaning light played over me, and many detached men who were not at all members of a unified whole stood, walked, ran around me. I stood up, I went with them, then you came toward me.

Leonhard: And when I stretched out my hand to you, you asked me: "Do you not also wonder, Leonhard?"

"About what?" I said.

And you: "About the theater . . ." and with that you smiled.

Then we spoke of other things, but I noticed that only your friendly feeling was with me and talked to me.

Daniel: Yes . . . for in the moment of my getting up it struck me, by chance but with seriousness, that I had to laugh at myself over what I had known all along and yet had not known: that most inclusive, most trivial reality which this theater was. That in the same moment as I and about me also these men on the stage, the actors, many detached men, not at all members of a unified whole, stood up, walked, ran, relaxed and made preparations; that today they had come out of their houses in the twilight in order to act, as we out of ours in order to watch; that that whole that had just now been, was the fictitious life of an evening, and this piece that had now taken place was the real life of the generations.

But when that had become present to me thus, it was suddenly no longer trivial, but very singular and thought-provoking. Like one who for many years had had a house and was glad of it without reflecting on it and all of a sudden it strikes him: "That is a house," and he smiles. But only now does it begin to dawn on him what that is: a house; or like one who for many years lived with a wife and shared a common life with her, and all of a sudden it strikes him: "That is a wife," and he smiles. But only now does it begin to dawn on him what that is: a wife. Thus I felt. For what sort of a reality was this here which so loose and playlike surrounded me? And what sort of an appearance was that there that so severely and totally admonished me? Which was the deeper reality: the act or the intermission? And what sort of a power was that which drew the men out of the broken, mediated, blunted polarity of their lives and placed them before the pure, strong, direct polarity of the tragedy? And who were they who "acted" this essential reality? What did they do when they acted it? These questions oppressed me when I spoke with you and I could not free myself from them. Indeed, I could not wish to do so. Thus, full of questions I returned to my place, and the third act of my drama commenced.

Over the boards strode, I know not why and whither, a maiden on slender brown feet. Then something strange happened to me. Whatever else the stage was vanished, and I saw what I had often thought of but had never seen: the maiden that in Indian villages represents the harvest goddess Gauri, Siva's consort. A bunch of wild mimosa was carried before her, she walked on slender brown feet through all the rooms of the houses, and at the threshold of each room she was asked the question: "Gauri, Gauri, from where do you come and what do you see?" I know not what she answered. But in the last room the mistress of the house bows before her, offers her sweet sacrificial food and speaks: "Come with golden feet and stay forever."

Leonhard: Is that not like the initiated saying to Mithras: "Remain with me in my soul"?

Daniel: Yes, so it is. But Gauri is *represented*. How is that done? This maiden represents Gauri.

Leonhard: Still not otherwise than a doll represents the one goddess. Whether the believer speaks to the statue of his God or the Indian wife to the living Gauri-doll, it is of the same nature; except that the divinity of the statue is probably believed in much more strongly than that of the maiden.

Daniel: That may be; but the statue presumably has no consciousness. What made me thoughtful was the consciousness of the maiden. It represents the goddess. To be sure, it does not "act" it. But is it not in its inactive feeling still somehow moved? Is not its sleep

112

blown by an incomprehensible breath of transformation?

Leonhard: Perhaps. But it does not do anything other than what is assigned to it.

Daniel: Are you so sure of that? That it does not hold the head a little more erect, hold the finger a little straighter, stretch the knee a little more tautly than otherwise? And is it ever assigned to a mortal being otherwise than as an ambiguous role that he must interpret with a single meaning in his action?

But my mind did not remain with Gauri. Once again before a curtain struck the stage, where a wedding had taken place, it wandered toward the north—or rather not so, instead it again emptied the stage and filled it with an ancient Nordic happening, and it too I saw only now. During the festive procession of Swedish peasants in which Freyr's statue is carried through the land along with that of the most beautiful virgin who is the bride of God, an unknown one breaks through and rides up to the holy carriage: similar to the God in shape, bearing, clothing, he receives the sacrificial offering of the people, marries the priestesses, blesses the land for fruitfulness. Gunnar Helming, an outlaw from Norway. He—played the God.

Leonhard: Yes, to deceive the faithful. This is the trick Jacob played on Esau.

Daniel: Do you think that Jacob and Gunnar deceived with slippery souls like shopkeepers? That under the animal hide and the God's

113

clothing the shudder of transformation did not overrun the body
clothed with deceit?

But again, called up by the wedding dance, a new play stood
before me: I saw the Bacchi on the stage. Not the Euripidean
poetic production: the old Dionysus play itself which represented
the *thiasos** and the nuptials, the passion and the resurrection of the
God, and the souls so shook in eternal movement that today a
grotesque rudiment still lives on in Thracian villages. I saw,
in front of the horse-eared Satyrs and the snake-adorned Bacchic
revelers, visible like a melodic column before the crudely shaped
pillars, the young man who had been selected and had prepared
himself to sacrifice his body for the body of the savior. Light and
detached he stood before the dark intoxication of his companions;
his foot struck the earth like the foot of a young steer; the streams
of pallor and of blood mixed themselves on his skin like fire and
water, and when his cheeks became red, they had the color of new
wine. In his eyes, however—which were not seeing, only existing
eyes—dwelt the transformations "to winds and waters and stars
and the birth of plants and animals," and his free limbs completed
it: freed from all conditioning, they moved gently, stood shining,
in space, took root and strove. I recognized with holy heart the
hero of the souls. And he, the youth, more ingenious than Gunnar
Helming and more believing than the Gauri-maiden—what was
it that happened to him? What was it that happened in him?
Did not the secret of magic rest on him to which all virginal
peoples are devoted: he who transforms himself into the God

---

* **Procession of persons dancing and singing in honor of Bacchus. [Translator]**

lives the life, does the deed, works the work of the God? Did he
not *realize* the God in and with his soul as in and with his body?

When that had become clear to me, the face disappeared, and I
again saw undivided the proceeding of the theater. But less still
than before did my glance want to follow this breadth. It clung
to one of the two protagonists who now stood to one side,
leaning against a solitary column, and regarded the tumult of the
wedding with folded arms. He was a man of high stature with a
wide chin and fine fingers. I gazed at him long and steadfastly;
something veiled his being from me; thus clouds lie around a cliff,
and a weak sun can only disperse them, not dissolve them.
And suddenly I saw, now fully clear and unveiled, *two* beings.
Neither of the two resembled the man whom I had just now
contemplated; both resembled him. They stood in a twofold light;
the one in an unearthly, flashing white, like glacier snow at
midday, the other in a bluish, weak light, like autumn hills in the
evening mist. The flashing one had a forehead of copper and
eyes of emerald; his mouth was firm as a stone bridge; his knee
arched like the knee of kings. The weak one had a forehead of
brass and eyes of opal; his mouth was stretched like a tightrope;
his knee stretched itself like the knee of a swimmer. The two
stood over against each other: I saw pole and opposite pole,
being and counterbeing in new form, and so keenly was I aware
of them that the hero at this hour could not be nearer my heart
than the actor.

Imagine a man, Leonhard, who breaks off his deed: who lives
only the soul's part of it, who feels that nameless spark, that kinesis

115

through which the deed from being the life-experience of an individual becomes a happening given to all: is he not similar to the doer and yet before all his counterpart? For this fragment of the deed that he lives receives the autonomy of a whole; it produces in his feeling the illusion of a wholeness because it satisfies his feeling; at first it was to him in its incompleteness a phantom and a terror, now it becomes for him the bread of life: from the fragment of the deed it becomes the simulacrum of the deed. The deed stands like a sign on the crossroads of the world; the simulacrum comes and vanishes on the plains of the soul. The deed emerges out of the darkness and is present, the simulacrum is foreknown and measured. There are, however, men in whom the existence which has not been worked out longs so strongly for fulfillment that no illusion lasts for them. They shatter on their contradiction, or the simulacrum becomes creative in them; they complete it—training and making manifest the gifts of their body, their voice, their system of movement—through images, representations, doubles of the deed. They act the kinesis; they free themselves in their acting. But they can only do this when they transform themselves: for Lyaeus[*] their God blesses them, he who can only bless for hours and ever again only for hours.

Leonhard: But are there not also other kinds and other ways?

Daniel: No matter what kind and no matter what way, the great, the genuine actor always stands over against the hero as the simulacrum the deed, as the possible the actual, as the ambiguous

---

[*] The releaser or deliverer from care, epithet of Bacchus. [Translator]

the simple, as the roaming the striding: polar. And this situation would be poisoned and nefarious if he sought to weaken the opposition; if he crept after and aped the hero. But precisely this he does not do; rather in all consecration of polar distance he stands over against the hero and—transforms himself into him. That is the paradox of the great actor. Freed, purified, transfigured in the transformation, he realizes the hero in ever-new uniqueness with his soul as with his body.

Leonhard: You say "the great actor." So what you say does not hold true for all?

Daniel: The little, the false actor, to whom the boldness of the simulacrum is alien, who stands over against the hero as the nothing stands opposite the something, fingers it with his senses; he collects the voice, the mien, the gestures of the hero; he traverses, explores, handles the world of the doer in order to acquire his material; and then constructs out of it a mask. But the great actor does not finger, he is transformed. Whether it is only the venturing genius of his simulacrum that helps him; whether it is demanded of him that he possess the hero in embryo in the all-possibility of his soul; whether, as I once dreamed it to myself, the daimon of an earlier life girdles and helmets him: the actor is transformed into the doer, the seeking into the acting, the wave into the way.

The great actor does not put on masks. In those formative hours in which he decisively lives his role, he penetrates—transforming himself, surrendering his soul and winning it back again—into the center of his hero and obtains from him the secret of the personal kinesis, the union of meaning and deed peculiar to him. Now he has the particular voice and gestures of the hero: because he has the element that commands and engenders them. He will become angry and bend forward, loose his scream; and noise and gesture are only in the timbre, their substance belongs to the man he plays, and only to him. Is he angry? He sounds the meaning of anger in himself, and the deed of anger resounds: because he has incarnated in himself their union, the personal kinesis.

Leonhard: So the actor does not really experience the agitations that he acts?

Daniel: He does not experience their feeling, but he experiences his action. And the excitement in which he stands is *his:* the excitement of the polarity, of the transformation. All high excitement has its origin in a polarity that is experienced, realized, carried out. Polarity is a task that can be carried out in many manners and on many ways. On whatever one this takes place— on the way of decision, on the way of inclusion, on the way of transformation—that high excitement which is above desire and pain, which is dearer and more sacred to the soul than desire and pain, bestows itself on the venturing man.

On whatever way it takes place. It may take place on the way of decision; that is the battle that is decided by genuinely faithful men on account of their desire for unity; decided acting—speaking —or keeping silent: so Francis of Assisi kept silent when the Spanish Dominic said to him, "Brother, I would that your rule and mine were one," and rejected the lower unity for the sake of the higher. Or it may take place on the way of inclusion; that is the love in which a genuinely present man embraces the creatures, so that he may live, remaining with himself in perfect power, the whistle of the tramp on his lips and the look of the fool in his eyes and, before he takes the poison drink, lament like Socrates the beautiful hair that the young Phaedo will sacrifice in mourning for him. Or it may take place on the way of transformation, that is, knowledge. For as the youth in the Bacchus play transforms himself into the God and realizes him, so the knower transforms himself into the world and realizes it. He cannot perceive its mystery with the senses nor inquire of it with thought; he can only penetrate it through transformation. Transformed, he executes with the movements of his existence the secret movement of the world: he lives the life of the world, he does its deed, he works its work—and so he knows it. For the secret of the world is the kinesis of the infinite, the union of meaning and being, and no one comes near it who reflects upon it: only he comes near it who does it; and he is the knower. He carries out the polarity in which he stands through realizing its opposite pole: through "finding" the meaning, as the Bacchic youth Dionysus and the actor the hero; the simulacrum that becomes creative in him is the imitation of the unknown God—which is realization. Thus through knowledge, as through conflict and through life, because a duality is fulfilled, unity is established out of it.

When I had become aware of this, I noticed that I no longer looked at the stage. I raised my eyes: there stood a man of high stature and looked, light and detached, after the departing wedding train.

Nothing any longer veiled from me his being; he was the son of venture and of polarity; and he was beautiful.

Over this picture fell the curtain for the third time. I leaned back, I was serene and thankful. And while I sat leaning back the wings of this undirected thankfulness bore me slowly through the world of the theater. But since it found no one here who could wholly bear it, it finally had to leave the theater and lift its flight into the hiddenness. On the border of dreams, where heaven and earth touch, it discovered the lonely wanderer for whom it was valid without his knowing it. All this time I had not thought of him, and yet it was his word that the actors spoke, his bidding that their gestures followed; Plato rightfully called them the messengers of the poets.

His word—his bidding—and yet: was it really his work that had been produced before me here, or had it not rather been transposed into another species, another law, another order? But on the other hand it seemed to me just therein a fulfillment of his primal deep intentions; as in every art, indeed, there dwell tendencies whose ripeness no longer finds room in this art and must seek or awaken another.

All poetry tends toward drama. Every lyric work is a dialogue the partner of which speaks in a superhuman language: what he says is the poet's secret. Every epic work is a dialogue in which the Fates speak along with the poet; to interpret for us their replies is the poet's task. The drama is pure dialogue; all feeling and all happening has in it become dialogue. It stands on the border of its art and points to that fulfillment and suspension in every other art in which the dialogue—is spoken.

It is he, the poet, who has made the actor speak. The strength of the poet is the word, the strength of the actor is the gesture; even speech is for him only a kind of gesture, and a later one. For among virginal peoples those who represent the divine wedding or the divine resurrection do not speak: they only dance; the aborigines on Swan River in Australia express the deepest truth of their souls when, to the surprise of the missionaries, they call the sacrament of the Last Supper a dance. And even at Eleusis only the hierophant spoke: until the poet came and released the voice of the actor for all time.

So I saw him, the master of the word, who moved the theater, and yet himself never really entered it. When the well-meaning light was extinguished and I knew: now the curtain will rise, I stood up and went softly out.

Leonhard: What, you did not see the last act of the play?

Daniel: I saw the last act of my drama. But how could I have remained? I had progressed with my thoughts to the border of dreams, to the poet; now I would be turned to and drawn away from the stage at the same time: to hear behind each word of each actor, even the most masterful, the gestureless, unaccented, untouched, the concise and secret, the essential-voiced word of the poem whose determined simplicity the splendid theater can only draw out, the faithful theater can only interpret; and behind the word of this poem the infinite word of the eternal poet would rustle for me, but not this or that and not all, rather the word of *the* poet: which I in this hour could only seek and will, but not behind the forms, rather in solitary spirit.

So I went out into the garden into whose mild darkness the moon-bow sent the arrow of a tender clearness. This pure light made me happy, this light that was neither lax nor severe but pure as the glance of a bird. Here I could think of the poet.

Of Enoch, who walked with Elohim, it is told that he had become one of the angels who was all eyes and wings. Thus is the poet. Everything in him perceives the things, and everything in him flies past the things. He is wholly in the one thing that he experiences, and yet is already and still in all the others at the same time. He knows the fervor of persevering like the painter and the fervor of soaring in air like the musician. His senses are the strongest anchor of the world, and his soul the most changeable keel. He drinks eternally, like the poet in the *Purgatorio*, out of both springs: Lethe and Mnemosyné, which Dante called Eunoe.

This duality in becoming of the poem appeared in new accent and effect. All action of man is, in fact, a mixture of creation and destruction, and every doer must, knowingly or unknowingly, reject the many that might arise through him for the sake of the one thing that he chooses; but this holds true of no one in so full a measure as the poet: because he incessantly decides. To write poetry is a choosing in the infinite; and this choosing is not a hunting, a seeking, a sifting, rather, it is a fire that has extinguishing and dissolving force. Each word of the poet is single; and yet there lies around each a ring of ungraspable material which represents the sphere of infinite vanishing; that is the track of the dissolving force of fire.

He whom Plato calls the messenger of the superpolar God is no less than this, the messenger of the polar earth. As in his deed the twofold stream that circulates in all living things manifests itself condensed and spiritualized, so there moves in his being, winged and aflame, all the tensions in which the soul of man erects itself, and every opposition, which otherwise is only sketched or blunted or accessible to mediation, is intensified in him to polarity. He knows the pole of exuberant strength and that of weakness, that of freedom and that of dependence, that of concentration and that of abandon, that of guilt and that of purity, that of form and that of formlessness: he recognizes them all in the world because he knows them in himself. Of Indra, the divine poet, who found in his songs dawn, sun, and fire, it is said that he holds all, embraces all, as the rim of the wheel embraces the spokes. Of the poet it can be said that his heart is the hub into which the spokes of polarities converge: here is not a suspension, however, but union, not indifference but fruitfulness. The poet bears the antitheses of the spirit, and in him they are fruitful. For he has a twofold great love: the love of the world in which everything that he experiences in himself as extreme and contradiction blooms toward him in the innermost truth of colors and tones as in a wonderful reconciliation, and the love of the word which, born out of the deep tension of earlier human dreams, shaped into the deep tension of seeking human generations, can redeem and

bring into harmony all tension. World and word: in the love
of the poet they come together, in the love of the poet their love
ascends, in their love all antitheses become fruitful. Fullness and
emptiness engender in the poet, pain and joy engender in the poet,
heaven and earth engender in the poet, word and world engender
in the poet. *To speak the world:* that builds the rainbow bridge
from pole to pole.

All poetry is dialogue: because all poetry is the shaping of a
polarity. The unmediated polarity of the soul, that is the lyric
situation: out of one of his pairs of opposites the poet has lifted
the one pole to the absolute and addresses it, treating himself as
the other pole. Or the mediated polarity of the world; that is the
epic situation: the poet subordinates his love for the world, and the
world ascends while the loving spirit stands over against it as
that reconciliation in which even the Fates do not terrify. Or the
dramatic: then the poet flings his burning contradiction into the
world, and it stands in flames.

The polarity which man experiences in himself wills unity.
And unity is not now or ever something which "is there"; unity
is that which eternally becomes. Not out of the world: out of our
action comes unity. The poet finds it where word and world
engender in him: in his work; there he grounds all duality in unity
But out of each work polarity arises for him anew: renewed.
Rejuvenated, sharpened, deepened, it summons him to new deed.

Thus the poet is the messenger of God and of the earth and is at
home in the two spheres. The force of fire is his force; it burns

in contradiction, and it shines in unity. Like Enoch, of whom a legend tells that he was transformed from flesh to fire; his bones are glowing coals, but his eyelashes are the splendor of the firmament.

V On Unity. Dialogue by the Sea

Lukas: It was a year ago today, Daniel, and that is the place where he climbed into his bark.

Daniel: Tell me how it happened.

Lukas: I had spoken to him in the evening. Rather, he had spoken to me. He stood by the sea, which was autumnal green and white as today, and looked with a still more tender gaze than usual at the water. Then he said: "Now the mother is free and no longer the maid of sun and heaven and may bear freely her own colors."

You must know, Daniel, that he never called the sea anything else than the mother.

Early next morning he climbed at the usual hour into his bark. The beach was deserted, but Kajetan, who at that time lived in the tower over there, saw through the glass the bark with the yellow sail slowly swimming out as always. It struck him that Elias was not bent forward as usual, even when the wind was favorable, but sat leaning back. He went below and asked the old Ubaldo what he expected the wind to be like; then he returned into the house and fussed a good while on a new violin that he had almost ready. It was for its sake that he had arisen so early. When he tried the tone he was dissatisfied, although the tone was beautiful; then the bark occurred to him again. He ran into the tower room, adjusted the glass, and saw the bark far out. Elias knelt on the edge of the bark, bent over, his arms extended perpendicular to the water; his two hands stroked it ever again like the limbs of a beloved being. Kajetan said to me that he had to think of Empedocles at that moment: with such movement of the hands he had always imagined Empedocles. That struck him so that he had to look away. When he looked again, Elias was no longer in the bark. Kajetan tore open the window, shouted something to the people below, which they did not understand, and ran down the stairs. It did not take long to send out a boat, but it took very long until they found the corpse. They tried in vain to awaken life in him.

Daniel: It touched you closely as though a friend of yours had died, and yet you hardly knew him.

128

Lukas: Who could have known him? . . . But, Daniel, never after the death of a friend have I experienced what I experienced here.

Of grief I felt nothing, and nothing of a desire that he might still spend life at my side. Rather his dying seemed to me right and well done. Also I did not think about the fact that he would be missing in my world; only that he had as yet been missing somewhere and now filled his place. The reality out of which he had once been broken in order that he might build himself a home in the formative might of two human bodies had remained incomplete until this moment when he returned, and now he entered into it and supplemented it again to its existence. Supplemented? No: fulfilled it. For he entered into it as a transformed one. Thirty years of earthly life—if there are also spirits, then they remain unnoticed as the fraction of a second is unnoticed by us—are a truth, and when a man has completed them, then they are the truth of truths. As a transformed one, as a completed one, one ripened to a transforming strength he returned, summoned to transform the mother herself. The old mystery shuddered through me out of the present. Was life a ripening and death the entrance into a sphere of divine deed before which earthly life only exists as a simile? But for whom could this hold true except only the completed man? Of those mythical creatures which are called cells it is said that most of those in our bodies perish and only a few become generative cells that have the capacity of living on. May we grasp this explanation of the living as a symbol of the superliving: are there also among men those who perish and those who ripen to eternity?

But as I thought this, it seemed to me suddenly as though I stood in Elias' bark and let down a sounding lead into the water, and my thoughts appeared to me an idle presumption, a *hybris* of unholy fantasy. Indeed, it was unholy to take away beforehand and forge an armor when he only fulfilled the direction of his highest hour, and dying genuinely carried through his life, when he entered the bottomless There naked and unarmed, without belief and without imagination, preserving only his readiness. I said to myself, There, and out of my own words the contradiction convulsively started up. How could there be a There if it was not also here? How could I become death's if I had not already now suffered it? My existence was no rolling ball that I could think of as stopping somewhere or preferably being thrown further. It was the bed in which two streams, coming from opposite directions, flowed to and in and over each other. There was not only in me a force that moved from the point of birth to the point of death or beyond; there was also a counterforce from death to birth, and each moment that I experienced as a living man had grown out of the mixture of the two—they mixed with each other like man and wife and created my being, and I never stood in the stream, but all the time in stream and opposing stream at once. What I *knew* was the stream coursing downward alone, but what I *was* comprehended the stream coursing downward and the stream coursing upward in one. A force bore me toward dying, and its flight I called time; but in my face blew a strange wind, and I did not know what name to give its flight. The two, whose vague image as it is projected into the shy mirror of our senses is called by us coming-to-be and passing-away, these two did not alternate with each other like building up and breaking down; they lay side by side in endless embrace, and each of my moments was their bed. It was foolish to wish to limit death to any particular moments of ceasing to be or of transformation; it was an ever-present might and the mother of being. Life engendered being, death received and bore it; life scattered its fullness, death preserved what it wished to retain. And this certitude was not unholy; it was, indeed, no feeling of being secure in any certainty but the unarmed trust in the infinite.

And this certitude, Daniel, I hold like the image of him who bequeathed it to me. But since I have again been on this beach and every yellow sail propounds to me anew the question of the world, a new unrest has come over me. For I feel morning after morning as though I journeyed out in Elias' bark, and those that once were enthroned for me in the poles of heaven, primally distant from each other so that my glance could never take in both of them at the same time, they sit quite near to me and to each other as fellows; with forehead bent forward the demon of life sits at the rudder and with head thrown back the goddess of death sits in the prow. Once it appeared enough to me to know about their existence—now that they have become familiar to me they have grown monstrous and agitating to my very heart: because I journey with them. From day to day the question mounts higher in me, what sort of a sea is it on which we travel, they and I, what sort of a sea has given birth to us, them and me. I know that in some way I am myself this sea, but I cannot reach there where I am it. And yet Elias reached there. Is what we call death, therefore, perhaps the way? To think that is senseless; what life did not accomplish, death too will not produce. Elias was *reached;* when he died, he expressed only the existing? But I? He is dead *for* me; how do I begin to live for him?

Once when they still appeared to me as boundaries, succeeding each other in service or play, these two satisfied me by their duality. Life handed me over to death as a letter that goes from runner to runner, life threw me to death like a torch that the hand touches only to fling it onward. It did not matter whether the receiver of the letter was near or far, it did not matter whether the torch moved into the infinite or was soon extinguished because of a sluggish player; it was simple and good to wander from life to death, and their doubleness was an ultimate and permanent state behind which I had no desire to look because it was the end and the consecration of my world. It has now become otherwise. Since these two are no longer boundaries but are in each other, since they are no longer over me but rule in me, an alternating movement no longer satisfies me; they drove me to penetrate behind them into the infinite that bears them both. As they work in me—through me—I listen, I am aware, I ask: what is the command? Now I know for certain that, destroying and shaping, they create my being, make out of what I actually am an essential being, and it did not occur to me to wish to know for what world of time or of eternity, of space or of spirit it is destined. But the unity that this creating commands and leads, that which bears life and death in right and left hand, that holy sea I want to know. I do not wish to grasp what is outside me, but I long to behold what I am.

Daniel: Let me tell you an event out of my youth. I was seventeen years old when a man died whom I had loved. Death laid itself about my neck like a lasso. It seized me as the Christian God seizes a sinner who must atone in God's place. That there was dying in the world had become my sin for which I had to do penance. Because of my isolation I could take no sleep and because of my disgust with living I could tolerate no nourishment; I believed that this happened as a penance. My family, strengthened by friends and physicians, regarded me fussily and helplessly as a changeling. Only my father met me with a calm, collected glance that was so strong that he reached my heart, inaccessible to all other perceptions. It was also this man, silent but united with the future, who soon came to the special decision through which I was saved: he sent me all alone into a secluded mountain place. I believe that the great time that I lived through there will return once more in the images of my dying hour. The first day in the face of the mountains crumbled my foolishness and threw it to the winds. The blue glow of the arch of heaven, the towering pride of the earth and the contacts with that infinite free being that we call air and of which only a shadow is accorded to us in the plains, surrounded me like a working divine power. Now for the the first time I recognized that I was separated; now for the first time I found myself before the eternal wall. And at the same time I knew that I could not come to my dead, not even through death, that he could not come to me, not even through birth; for I saw the deeds of the world on another level than that of the proclaimed truths. In the feeling that this knowledge was full, I now lived through the days, without consolation, but no longer losing myself as in the penance, rather winning myself through despair. For despair, Lukas, is the highest of God's messengers; it trains us into spirits that can create and decide.

One morning I had climbed a small Alp from which one looked down on an equally small lake enclosed by crags. This lake received my whole gaze and held it like a magic crystal. Soon the surrendered gaze was freighted with my forces and my movement. Relaxing I felt how everything in me went into it; it grew as I waned; and finally even the living power of grief, my orphaned state, went out of me—I was as little orphaned now as a newborn child whose mother has died. Thus I fell asleep. I still knew my glance to be hovering over the deep, then this too disappeared before the consuming nothingness. I slept in the timeless while the happening of the world meted out my hours.

The first thing that I sensed on awaking was a terrible, absurd, penetrating question about the lake. And yet—this was my next perception—yet I saw; but I saw nothing isolated any longer: I did not look. The power of selection of my glance had deserted me; I saw everything as a cloudy image in which all separateness dissolved. Light and dark were entangled in each other; all shape had stepped out of its boundaries and exploded into the iridescent snake-coil of the colors which had enclosed the spectral horizon. Fleeing from the unformed world, I relied upon my body and knew it as an island in the torrent of annihilations. Its firm being rested, bound and formed, in the midst of chaos, and yet in the most remarkable way was shattered and deformed by all things in its firmness. Instead of the streaming simplicity of the lived human image I found a twofoldness in myself: one half of me was life, the other had become death; in both I experienced not states

134

but powers, here the command of the surging blood, there the compulsion of passing away. And while the movement of formation stormed through the one level, the spasm of disintegration jerked through the other. Both were so intensified to the uttermost, however, that my feeling lay below like an anvil and suffered the twofold hammer blows. And there, Lukas, at the uttermost, my soul arose in me. Not that seeming soul that thinks of self-preservation but the caretaker that wants completion. It trembled violently under the abomination of my cleavage and longed to go into the world in order to bring me unity. But in all the world it found only mixture and confusion, not unity. Then my body was inspired and did the simple deed: my two arms raised themselves, my hands bent to each other, my fingers entwined, and over all horror there arched the God-powerful bridge. Then my body became united, the world became one for me, my sight returned to me unburdened: free and unencumbered I lay and looked at the lake, which looked at me. And in this doubly united gaze of giving and receiving I perceived that I was no longer separated. I had torn down the eternal wall, *the wall within me*. From life to death—from the living to the dead flowed the deep union. I could not come to my dead, nor he to me, but we were united like the eye and the lake: because I was united in myself.

In that hour, Lukas, the teaching came to me: the one thing that is needful. It came to me mute and concealed, like the grain of seed in the earth; it laid itself on my breast and remained with me. I had it from that time on, but I did not know it. On all wanderings I sensed its presence, but I was not aware of it and had to march from every journey into a new one. Until in a later hour I marked that I had experienced it, without anything happening other than that a moment joined itself to a moment, even as what a little while ago was a bud in full readiness is now a flower that has opened.

Since then I understood, Lukas: he who genuinely experiences the world experiences it as duality. He looks at it neither with that close glance of the woman who cherishes the little multiplicity of an enclosed foreground nor with that distant glance of the man who subordinates the things in the wave of a broad dynamic; he looks at it with the glance of the human being: he grasps and decides and brings forth out of the play of the manifold the essential line of tension. And to overcome this tension in his task.

The duality is many-named and multiform; differently known, it is different in circumference and significance; it remains the same in the tension. All wisdom of the ages has the duality of the world as its subject; its point of departure is to know it, its goal to overcome it. However it names the two forces that it makes known—spirit and matter, form and material, being and becoming, reason and will, positive and negative element, or with any of the other pair of names—it has in mind the overcoming of their tension, the unification of their duality. It seeks this through many ways, but none of its ways can satisfy him who is faithful to the totality of his life-experience. The longing for unity is the glowing ground of the soul, but he feels that he would degrade this longing if he surrendered something of the fullness of his life-experience to please it. He can only become obedient to it in truth if he serves it out of his completeness, strives to fulfill it out of his completeness, and thus preserves the experienced duality undiminished in the force of its distance. Therefore, none of the ways that the wisdom of the ages takes can satisfy him. That unity for the sake of which he must drown out the powerful voices of duality is not the right one for him; the tensions that he experienced in the storm he does not desire to do away with but to embrace. They have sketched his life with the diagram of greatness; only in them, out of them, with them can he penetrate to the greatest.

Each of the ways that the wisdom of the ages takes and that the seeker follows has become a wrong way for him; he must forsake each because he knows that to follow them he would have to forsake himself, the mystery of his life-experience. And so he wanders from way to way until in a later hour he comes upon the simple path of his self which is ready for him.

A wrong way, Lukas, was that sublime wisdom which commanded one to strip off the world of duality as the world of appearance, "like a snake skin," and to enter the world of unity, or rather to recognize himself as standing in it, as being it. For the faithful man wants to find it as just this human being who lives through the whole swinging of duality, who receives and endures its fearful blessing. What does it matter to him henceforth that this is the world of illusion? He has measured its depths and may no longer deny his measure. Henceforth he will not retreat before the fluctuating, raging, whirling world of division and of contradiction; he will stand steadfast therein, in the midst of it stand steadfast and dare just out of it to derive and create unity. He will not go again into the wilderness where one needs only to annihilate in order to find; he does not want to annihilate but to fulfill, and he would rather renounce salvation than to exclude Satan's kingdom from it. Not behind the world but in the world will his unity be sought, for what he seeks is not overcoming but completion, and he who completes cannot desire to obliterate anything, to weaken anything, to equalize anything.

And also a wrong way to the faithful man, Lukas, was that upright wisdom that thought duality together into unity. I mean those whose clear meaning it was to see the two forces together, no matter in what form they appear, as sides, as faces, as aspects and over the abyss of duality to let the glory of identity shine forth. This way, too, did not satisfy the faithful man. For if I perhaps know that nature and idea are manifestations of one single reality, is that reality then directly present to me as unity, present in the midst of the elemental tension of nature and idea that shatters my firm heart? Or if I perhaps know that action and passion are expressions of a single basic process, can it ever give and reveal itself to me in the face of the hard gift and revelation of those two which circle my fluctuating life like light and darkness? I will honor them, these genuine thinkers, as I honor those who have genuinely put aside becoming, but I will not take their way. For their way leads aside from the clattering highway on which I live and outside of which I will not accept God.

Therefore, Lukas, the third way could also not benefit the faithful one: that innermost wisdom that proclaims that the awakened man indifferentiates all opposites and all antinomies in himself. For like

138

the suspension and the equalization, neutrality also cannot be unity for him. If the being of the world were perhaps designated as the one end and the not-being or becoming of the world as the other and the lived truth of the awakened man were set in the middle, then this might well mean salvation from suffering. But he who loses the ends and the swinging suffering has lost the flight and the song of his life, the noble material of completed unity. If I were a bird, says the faithful man, then I would not have life in my belly but in my wings, and not in my balancing but in my soaring. Or if I were a bell clapper, then I would want to be aware of my soul when, ringing on my walls, I touched one of them, not when I withstood them both. For his place is not in compromise, but in decision, and as precious as the silence of heaven is to him, more precious to him still is the organ playing of earth.

And yet, Lukas, each of the three wrong ways produced truth in the faithful one, each ripened a layer of teaching in him to conscious being. The first confirmed in him the striving for unity, for what he beheld detached guaranteed him fulfillment: what yielded itself to him in the formless depths that *was,* and because it was, it must also arise for him out of the formed breadths; what revealed itself to him in self-collectedness must prove itself true for him in the scattered totality of his life-experience; to that which he had unbecome out of the world, to just that he must be able to become in the world—then only was what he sought genuine.

And then came the second way and radiated unity for him over the world, joined might to might and let them cleave to each other like lovers, no, as the hollow of the bow cleaves to its curve. Thus it was recognized, known, and thought, but it was not reality for it was not lived. But unity must be able to be lived, to be *realized*.

The third way undertook to realize it. All duality was tested in its own being and unity sought with the whole attitude of life in the world. But because the search took place not in the extended swinging, but in the indifference, what was won was not unity fulfilled by all-being but the independence of zero. The awakened man is independent of all, not at one with all. The genuine, completed unity can be nothing other than the man all of whose tension is unified and in whom the world unifies all its tension.

And now I shall tell you, Lukas, how the final level of the teaching ripened in me and how the teaching arose. But there is almost nothing more to tell. I said it to you already, in fact: a moment joined itself to a moment. On a gloomy morning I walked upon the highway, saw a piece of mica lying, lifted it up and looked at it for a long time; the day was no longer gloomy, so much light was caught in the stone. And suddenly as I raised my eyes from it, I realized that while I looked I had not been conscious of "object" and "subject"; in my looking the mica and "I" had been one; in my looking I had tasted unity. I looked at it again, the unity did not return. But there it burned in me as though to create. I closed my eyes, I gathered in my strength, I bound myself with my object, I raised the mica into the kingdom of the existing. And there, Lukas, I first felt: *I,* there I first was I.

The one who looked had not yet been I; only this man here, this unified man, bore the name like a crown. Now I perceived that first unity as the marble statue may perceive the block out of which it was chiseled; it was the undifferentiated, I was the unification. Still I did not understand myself; but then there flashed through me the memory: thus had my body fifteen human years before done the simple deed and, the fingers entwined, united life and death to "I."

True unity cannot be found, it can only be created. He who creates it realizes the unity of the world in the unity of his soul. Thus beforehand he must live through the tension of the world in his soul as his own soul's tension.

Whenever the living soul experiences itself, it experiences itself as duality. Its unity is only a name, its multiplicity only an image; in all its movement, in all its perceptions it experiences itself as duality, tension, task. Knowing and feeling, acting and valuing, man stands in the protean phenomenon of the inner polarity in which the one pole is always directly present to him, the other indirectly, the one is possessed by him, the other is known about. Thus in him the tension is made ready which he shall broaden to the all-tension. The inner polarity is the vessel that is filled with the smallest content and yet can contain the infinite: he who wills to create unity fills it with infinity.

He takes the tension of the world upon himself so that it is lived by his soul as its own. He takes upon himself, say, the tension of spirit and matter, and the soul experiences world-wide its own

freedom and its own bondage, its own spontaneity and its own
being conditioned, its own bearing and its own being borne.
It is no longer so that the one pole is present, the other only
known about, but in it there takes place simultaneously the full
polarity in undiminished brilliance and strength. The man takes
the tension of material and form upon himself, and the soul
experiences world-wide its own wildness and its own taming,
its own fullness and its own shape, its own chaos and its own
cosmos. It comprehends in itself action and suffering at once, and
the stream between the two that streams through it is the stream
of the eternal powers. The man takes upon himself the tension
of being and becoming, and the soul experiences world-wide its
own stillness and its own movement, its own fixity and its own
whirl, its own continuance and its own transformation. The two
aspects of the great nature stand with each other in the outstretched
heaven of the living soul. Thus the world lives its duality from
within: in the man who wills to create the unity.

He creates it by bringing together in himself the tension that
he has taken upon him: *by awakening the I of this tension.*

There is in reality no I except the I of a tension: in which it brings
itself together. No pole, no force, no thing—only polarity,
only stream, only unification can become I.

Look before you, Lukas: it is ebb tide. Can the ebb tide say I?
Or the flood tide? But imagine the sea to have a spirit that
comprehends in itself the unity of ebb and flood: it could say I.

The mica could not say it; he who looked at it could not say it; and the undifferentiated of its first look was only material. But when it had brought its tension together, the unified could say I.

What we commonly mean by "I" is a starting point and expedient, a grammatical fact. But the I of the tension is work and reality.

We live so much the more really, so much the more individually the greater tension we realize as "I." In this increasing measure the I comes into being in us.

To live the tension of the world is the highest test of our being.

Experiencing freedom and bondage in one as one's own, the soul brings forth the I that embraces freedom and bondage as its functions. Fulfilling timelessly the swinging of fullness and form, the soul summons the I that bears fullness and form as its limbs. Uniting continuance and transformation in the all-present, the soul awakens the I that possesses continuance and transformation as its gestures.

This I is the I of the world. In it unity is fulfilled. And this I is inextricably inserted in a human life. Human life cannot escape the conditioned. But the unconditioned stands ineffaceably inscribed in the heart of the world.

The sum of a life is the sum of its unconditionedness. The might of a life is the might of its unity. He who dies in the completed unity of his life utters the I that is not inserted, that is the naked eternity.

We spoke of death, my friend Lukas; we have all the time spoken of nothing else. You wish to know the holy sea, the unity that bears life and death in right and left hand. You cannot know it otherwise than when you take upon yourself the tension of life and death and live through the life and death of the world as your life and your death. Then the I of this tension will awaken in you—the unconditioned, the unity of life and death.

About the Author

Martin Buber was born in Vienna in 1878. His youth was spent in the home of his grandfather, the great rabbinic scholar, Solomon Buber, where he made contact with numerous Hasidic communities of Galicia. The years from 1897 to 1923 saw him engaged in Zionist activities, in the editorial direction of *Der Jude*, and in the writing of his works on mysticism, Hasidism, and the transitional works that prepared the way for *I and Thou* (1923). From 1923 to 1933 Buber taught Jewish Philosophy of Religion at the University of Frankfurt am Main, and in 1925, with Franz Rosenzweig, he commenced a new German translation of the Hebrew Bible. In 1938, Buber left Germany for Israel, where he served as Professor of Social Philosophy at the Hebrew University in Jerusalem until his retirement in 1951. Honored throughout the world, Martin Buber has recently completed the translation of the Bible into German which he and Rosenzweig began almost forty years ago.

DANIEL by Martin Buber
was designed and illustrated
by Joseph del Gaudio.